^A*Style* MANUAL *for* COMMUNICATION MAJORS

FIFTH EDITION

John Bourhis
Carey Adams
Southwest Missouri State University

Scott Titsworth
Moorehad State University

The McGraw-Hill Companies, Inc.
Primis Custom Publishing

*New York St. Louis San Francisco Auckland Bogotá
Caracas Lisbon London Madrid Mexico Milan Montreal
New Delhi Paris San Juan Singapore Sydney Tokyo Toronto*

McGraw-Hill Higher Education

A Division of The *McGraw-Hill* Companies

A Style **MANUAL** *for* **COMMUNICATION MAJORS**

McGraw-Hill's Primis Custom Publishing consists of products that are
produced from camera-ready copy. Peer review, class testing, and
accuracy are primarily the responsibility of the author(s).

 2 3 4 5 6 7 8 9 0 CUS CUS 9 0 9

Part Number 0-07-228684-9 of Set Number ISBN 0-07-228934-1

Editor: Dee Renfrow
Printer/Binder: Book-Mart Press, Inc.

Contents

PREFACE

The goal of this manual is simple yet ambitious. <u>A Style Manual for Communication Majors</u> is designed to reduce the number of errors made by students in their formal academic writing. It emerged out of our increasing frustration with our students' inability to communicate their thoughts and feelings effectively in written form. The frighteningly typical response to our instruction that students select any formal writing style for preparing their written assignments is blank stares and incomprehension. We might as well be speaking a foreign language when we mention <u>AP</u>, <u>APA</u>, <u>MLA</u>, or <u>Chicago Manual of Style</u>. We are convinced that either students are not receiving the instruction they need elsewhere or they forget most of what they are taught by the time they take courses in the major. Whatever the cause, the result is the same — most of our undergraduate majors do not know, understand and/or use the rules for writing formal academic papers.

There is an extensive body of literature in our discipline which indicates that the ability to communicate effectively in writing and orally will play a decisive role in the career success of our students once they graduate. One of the authors can recall a student, who after receiving a failing grade on a written assignment because she had made 72 spelling, punctuation, grammatical, and format errors in a seven page paper, responded, "I don't know why this writing stuff is so important. When I graduate I'll have a secretary who will do all this stuff for me!" More recently, one of the authors served on a university-wide committee that was responsible for selecting students to receive university scholarships. An alarming number of very bright, highly motivated students, with otherwise impressive applications did not receive support because they had made careless spelling, punctuation and grammatical errors in putting together their applications. Spelling, punctuation and grammar, as well as attention to detail and following conventions do have real world consequences. Despite our best efforts to describe the "real world" to such students, we fear some are destined for graduate work in the school of hard knocks.

<u>A Style Manual for Communication Majors</u> is designed to supplement whatever texts you currently use, in whatever courses you are currently taking or teaching. It contains condensed versions of the two most commonly used writing styles in our discipline (<u>MLA</u> and <u>APA</u>) and full text examples written by undergraduate students on topics that will be of interest to students. Because the conventions have been condensed to include only those most commonly needed by undergraduates, students will find this style guide more accessible and less intimidating. In this case, we believe less is more. If you

intend to pursue advanced work in the discipline, we encourage you to purchase the complete copies of both the MLA and APA style manuals.

The fifth edition of A Style Manual for Communication Majors contains the following features to help students write formal papers:

- Condensed versions of the most recent editions of the Modern Language Association Handbook for Writers of Research Papers and the Publication Manual of the American Psychological Association.
- Current examples drawn from national and regional journals, leading texts and key works in the field of Communication.
- Full text examples of papers written in MLA and APA-style documentation.
- Full text example of an annotated list of references.
- Clear and concise rule boxes that highlight key conventions in both MLA and APA-style documentation.
- A revised chapter on using paper and electronic indexes to access the available published literature in Communication.
- A revised discussion on how to cite electronic sources of information in both MLA and APA-style documentation.
- A revised chapter devoted to critical evaluation and selection of supporting material, especially Internet-based sources.

John Bourhis, Carey Adams and Scott Titsworth
June 1999

CHAPTER ONE
A CONDENSED MLA STYLE GUIDE

FORMATTING THE TEXT OF YOUR PAPER

TYPING

Unless otherwise instructed, all written work submitted for evaluation must be typed. The type must be clear, dark, and easily readable. Laser quality output has become the minimum acceptable standard for instructors as well as prospective employers. Use only standard typefaces such as Courier, Prestige Elite, Helvetica or Times Roman or their equivalents, and standard type sizes (ten or twelve point). Only type on one side of the paper. Never use "fancy" or unusual fonts. Do not justify the right margin.

PAPER

Use only heavy (twenty pound or heavier) white, 8½ by 11 inch bond paper. Never submit any work typed on erasable or "onion skin" paper. If you use erasable paper, have a high-quality photocopy made on heavy white, 8½ by 11 inch bond paper and submit the photocopy to your instructor. Keep the original copy for your files.

MARGINS

Leave one-inch margins at the top, bottom, left, and right of your paper. Nothing should appear within this one-inch margin except pagination. Indent the first word of each paragraph five spaces from the left margin and set-off quotations ten spaces from the left margin. Do not indent the first word of a set-off quotation. A set-off quotation is any quotation of more than four typed lines. Do not justify the right margin.

LINE SPACING

Your paper should be double-spaced throughout, including the heading, title, text, quotations, and works cited.

TITLE PAGE

Unless otherwise instructed to provide one, <u>MLA</u> does not require a formal, separate title page. Instead, type your name, your instructor's name, the course name and number, and the date at the top of the first page — flush with the left margin. Note that <u>MLA</u> follows the (day month year) format. Type and center the title of the paper two spaces below the heading. Double-space between the title and the first line of the text of the paper. If your instructor specifically requires that you have a formal, separate title page for your paper, follow the model on the following page. If you are required to provide a formal title page, do not repeat the author, instructor, course and date information that appears on the formal title page on the first page of the text of the paper. Repeat the title of the paper and double-space to the first line of text.

Wagon 1

Chuck Wagon
↕ 2 spaces
Dr. Lynn Harter
↕ 2 spaces
Organizational Communication 336
↕ 2 spaces
12 September 1999
↕ 2 spaces
Self-Disclosure Among Dual Career Couples
↕ 2 spaces

Increasingly, dual-career couples have become the norm in our

society rather than the exception. Unfortunately, relatively little is

known about the communication patterns between dual-career couples.

Self-Disclosure Among Dual Career Couples

M
L
A

Chuck Wagon

Organizational Communication 336

Dr. Lynn Harter

12 September 1999

PAGINATION

All scholarly writing requires pagination. Number each of the pages consecutively throughout the manuscript. Place all pagination in the upper right-hand corner, ½ inch from the top and ½ inch from the right of the page. Include your last name preceding each page number. Do not punctuate the page number in any way. The first page of the manuscript is the page on which the text of the manuscript begins. A formal title page is not counted as a page of the manuscript.

⇕ ½ inch from top

Wagon 2

⇕ ½ inch

First line of the text on the page appears ½ inch below the

pagination for the page for a total top margin of 1 inch.

SAMPLE MLA ENTRIES

1.0   BOOKS

The basic format for a book entry includes: author's name; title of part of book; title of the book; editor, translator, or compiler; edition; place of publication; publisher; and date of publication.

1.1   One Author

Northouse, Peter. <u>Leadership: Theory and Practice</u>.

Thousand Oaks: SAGE Publications, 1997.

Kanter, Rosabeth. <u>Men and Women of the Corporation</u>. New

York: Basic Books, 1977.

1.2   Two or Three Authors

Kotter, John and James Heskett. <u>Corporate Culture and</u>

<u>Performance</u>. New York: The Free Press, 1992.

1.3   Four or More Authors

Brilhart, John et al. <u>Practical Public Speaking</u>. New York:

HarperCollins Publishers, 1993.

Frey, Lawrence et al. <u>Investigating Communication: An</u>

<u>Introduction to Research Methods</u>. Englewood Cliffs:

Prentice Hall, 1991.

▲ *How do I know which words to capitalize in the title of a book?*

In book titles and subtitles, capitalize the first word, the last word, and all principal words. Capitalize all nouns, pronouns, adjectives, and adverbs. Do not capitalize coordinating conjunctions (and, but, for, nor, or) or prepositions introducing phrases (of, before, in, to). Do not capitalize an article (a, an, the) unless it is the first word in a title. Separate titles from subtitles with a colon and capitalize the first word after the colon. Include any other punctuation that is part of the title.

1.4   Two or More Books by the Same Author

Bales, Robert. <u>Interaction Process Analysis: A Method for the</u>

<u>Study of Small Groups</u>. Reading: Addison-Wesley

Publishing Company, 1950.

---. <u>Personality and Interpersonal Behavior</u>. New York: Holt,

Rinehart and Winston, 1970.

M
L
A

1.5   Book with an Editor

Collins, Randall, Ed. <u>Three Sociological Traditions: Selected</u>

<u>Readings</u>. New York: Oxford University Press, 1985.

1.6   Book with Two Editors

Knapp, Mark, and Gerald Miller, Eds. <u>Handbook of</u>

<u>Interpersonal Communication</u>. Beverly Hills: Sage

Publications, 1985.

Putnam, Linda, and Michael Pacanowsky, Eds.

<u>Communication and Organizations: An Interpretive</u>

<u>Approach</u>. Beverly Hills: Sage Publications, 1983.

1.7   An Edition Other than the First

Babbie, Earl. <u>Survey Research Methods</u>. 2nd ed. Belmont:

Wadsworth Publishing Company, 1997.

Vogt, Paul. <u>Dictionary of Statistics and Methodology: A</u>

<u>Nontechnical Guide for the Social Sciences</u>. 2nd ed.

Thousand Oaks: SAGE Publications, 1999.

1.8   A Work in a Book

Redding, Charles. "Stumbling Toward Identity: The

Emergence of Organizational Communication as a Field

of Study." <u>Organizational Communication: Traditional</u>

<u>Themes and New Directions</u>. Eds. Robert McPhee and

Phillip Tompkins. Beverly Hills: Sage Publications,

1985. 15-54.

▲ *Note:*

> The page numbers at the end of the citation indicate the first
> and last pages of the work in a book. Type two-digit page
> numbers as they appear in the article. If the first two digits
> of three-digit page numbers are identical, delete the first
> digit of the second page number (201-02). If the first two
> digits of four digit page numbers are identical, delete the
> first two digits of the second page number (1112-13).

1.9   A Translation

> Aristotle. <u>The Rhetoric</u>. Trans. W. Rys Roberts. New York:
>
> Modern Library, 1954.
>
> Cicero. <u>Rhetorica ad Herennium</u>. Trans. Harry Caplan.
>
> Cambridge: Harvard University Press, 1954.

2.0   ARTICLES

The basic format for an article entry includes: author's name; title of
article; name of periodical; volume number; date of publication; and
page numbers. The page numbers at the end of the citation indicate the
first and last pages of the article. Type two-digit page numbers as they
appear in the article. If the first two digits of three-digit page numbers
are identical, delete the first digit of the second page number (201-02).
If the first two digits of four digit page numbers are identical, delete
the first two digits of the second page number (1112-13).

2.1   One Author

> Asker, Barry. "Student Reticence and Oral Testing: A Hong
>
> Kong Study of Willingness to Communicate."
>
> <u>Communication Research Reports</u> 15 (1999): 162-168.

▲ *How do I know which words to capitalize in article and journal titles?*

Follow the rules for capitalizing words in book titles.

2.2   Two or Three Authors

Ayres, Joe and Brian Heuett. "The Relationship Between

Visual Imagery and Public Speaking Apprehension."

Communication Reports 40 (1997): 87-94.

Kramer, Michael, Ronda Callister, and Daniel Turban.

"Information-Receiving and Information-Giving During

Job Transitions." Western Journal of Communication 59

(1995): 151-170.

2.3   Four or More Authors

Buller, David et al. "Interpersonal Deception: I. Deceivers'

Reactions to Receivers' Suspicions and Probing."

Communication Monographs 58 (1991): 1-24.

Kreps, Gary et al. "Applied Communication Research:

Scholarship That Can Make a Difference." Applied

Communication Research 19 (1991): 71-87.

2.4   Monthly or Bimonthly Periodical

Erbe, Bonnie. "Madame President?" Working Woman June

1999: 24.

2.5   Weekly or Biweekly Periodical

Cloud, John. "Just a Routine School Shooting." <u>Time</u> 15 (31

May 1999): 34-43.

▲ *When citing an article in a periodical, when do I use quotation marks and when do I underline?*

Place the full title of an article in quotation marks. Put the appropriate concluding punctuation before the closing quotation mark. Underline the name of the periodical.

3.0   NEWSPAPERS

The basic format for a newspaper entry includes: author's name; article title; name of newspaper; date; and page.

3.1   Signed Article from a Daily Newspaper

Mann, William. "Mistakes in Air War Hurt NATO." <u>The</u>

<u>Kansas City Star</u> 24 May 1999: 1.

Bearak, Barry. "Frozen in Fury at the Roof of the World."

<u>The New York Times</u> 23 May 1999: 1.

3.2   Unsigned Article from a Daily Newspaper

"Reno Should Resign Over Spy Scandal, Senators Say."

<u>USA Today</u> 24 May 1999: 1.

3.3   Signed Editorial from a Daily Newspaper

Squires, Lauren. "Don't Be Afraid of Not Knowing."

Editorial. <u>Springfield News Leader</u> 24 May 1999: 6A.

Shapiro, Walter. "Kosovo's Plight is Unbelievable Yet

Undeniable." Editorial. <u>USA Today</u> 24 May 1999: 15A.

3.4   Unsigned Editorial from a Daily Newspaper

"Airline Tactics Fair?" Editorial. <u>Springfield News Leader</u>

24 May 1999: 7A.

4.0   UNPUBLISHED MANUSCRIPT

Bourhis, John."Classrooms Without Walls: The Future of Internet-

based Instruction." Unpublished Manuscript, 1999.

5.0   UNPUBLISHED PAPERS PRESENTED AT MEETINGS

Stewart, Catherine and Carey Adams. "Communication Style, Leader-

member Exchange, and Communication Satisfaction." National

Communication Association, Nov., 1997, Chicago.

6.0   PERSONAL INTERVIEWS

The basic format for a personal interview includes: interviewees'
name; the kind of interview conducted (Personal interview or
Telephone interview); and date.

Berquist, Charlene. Telephone interview. 25 Jan.1999.

Dillon, Randy, and Gloria Galanes. Personal interview. 1 Feb.1999.

7.0   LECTURES

The basic format for a lecture includes: lecturer's name; title of lecture;
the sponsoring organization or meeting; place where lecture was
delivered; and date. If there is no title use an appropriate descriptive
label (Lecture, Address, Speech, Presentation).

Allen, Mike. "Statistics for Dummies." University of Wisconsin at

Milwaukee, Milwaukee. 1 Sept. 1999.

CHAPTER ONE

Tkachuk, Henry. "Losing Fishing Strategies for Northern Pike."

Concordia College, Moorhead. 5 Jan. 1999.

8.0   TWO OR MORE LECTURES BY THE SAME SOURCE

Bourhis, John. "Origins of Classical Theory." Southwest Missouri

State University, Springfield. 15 Jan. 1999.

---. "Systems Theory." Southwest Missouri State University,

Springfield. 10 Feb. 1999.

---. "Weick's Model of Organizing." Southwest Missouri State

University, Springfield. 15 Feb. 1999.

9.0   FILMS

The basic format for a film includes: title of film; director; distributor; and year. You may include other data that is pertinent.

The Four Seasons. Dir. Alan Alda. With Alan Alda, Carol Burnett,

Len Carious, Sandy Dennis, Rita Moreno, Jack Weston, and Bess

Armstrong. Universal, 1981.

The Breakfast Club. Dir. John Hughes. With Emilio Estevez, Judd

Nelson, Molly Ringwald, Anthony Hall, and Ally Sheedy.

Universal, 1985.

10.0   TELEVISION PROGRAMS

The basic format for a television program includes: program title; network; local station on which you saw the program; the city; and date of broadcast. Include the episode or segment title if readily available.

CBS Evening News. CBS. KOLR, Springfield. 25 Oct. 1999.

CNN Headline News. CNN. CNN, Springfield. 16 Jan. 1999.

M
L
A

11.0   RADIO BROADCASTS

The basic format for a radio broadcast includes: program title; network; local station on which you heard the program; the city; and date of broadcast.

All Things Considered. NPR. KSMU, Springfield. 24 Oct. 1999.

Morning Edition. NPR. KSMU, Springfield. 2 Jan. 1999.

CITING SOURCES IN THE TEXT OF YOUR PAPER

MLA style uses parenthetical references for citing sources. Parenthetical references are placed within the text of the paper rather than at the bottom of each page (footnotes) or at the end of the paper (endnotes). The basic format for an MLA parenthetical reference is: (author's last name, followed by a space and the page(s) upon which the cited information can be found). For example:

Native English speakers tend to receive significantly higher scores on

The Speaking Proficiency English Assessment Kit (SPEAK) than

non-native English speakers (Powell 40).

▲ *When must I document a source?*

You must document a source whenever you:
1. directly quote, word-for-word, someone else's work;
2. paraphrase or summarize someone else's work; and
3. use facts and data that are not common knowledge.

CHAPTER ONE

As a way of adding variety to your citations, mention the author's name in the text and cite the page number parenthetically. For example:

> Powell demonstrated that native English speakers tend to receive
>
> significantly higher scores on The Speaking Proficiency English
>
> Assessment Kit (SPEAK) than non-native English speakers (40).

When citing an entire work, the most elegant citation is to include the author (and possibly the work) in the text and omit the parenthetical reference entirely.

> In <u>Thriving on Chaos: Handbook for a Management Revolution</u>, Tom
>
> Peters shatters many of the conventional myths regarding effective
>
> management.

or

> Peters shatters many of the conventional myths regarding effective
>
> management.

Follow the same rules for citing a direct quotation.

> "In general, the present findings suggest that little has changed over the
>
> past thirty years in the textbook treatment of communication
>
> apprehension" (Pelias 51).

The same rules apply when citing a source with two or three authors.

> "It is our belief and the belief of perspective employers throughout the
>
> United States that courses such as public speaking, listening, and
>
> interpersonal communication should be included as an oral
>
> communication core in such a blended program" (Curtis, Winsor, and
>
> Stephens 13).

When citing a work with more than three authors, name the first author and include the abbreviation "et al." (meaning "and others") followed by a space and page number(s).

> "Authority, personal experience, intuition, custom, and magic may be
>
> good starting points for the systematic pursuit of knowledge, but they
>
> don't necessarily lead to valid knowledge about the world" (Frey et al.
>
> 6).

When a direct quotation exceeds four typed lines in length, MLA requires that the quotation be "set-off" from the rest of the text. Introduce and cite the quotation as you would normally, omit the quotation marks, indent the entire quotation ten spaces from the left margin, and write it in block form within the text. For example:

This particular study raises a number of issues that have heuristic

value.

> The anxiety actually experienced during the communication
>
> event was not thought to affect the CA trait. In fact, reducing CA
>
> was discussed in terms of clinical treatment such as systematic
>
> desensitization. The results of the present study indicate that
>
> communication state anxiety experiences could reduce trait CA.
>
> (McCroskey et al. 181-2)

▲ *Note* that the appropriate punctuation for a block quotation goes at the end of the last word of the quotation, not at the end of the citation. Do not include any punctuation at the end of the citation.

When citing a single work by an author of two or more works in the text of your paper, include the author's last name followed by a comma and the complete title (if relatively short) or an abbreviated version of the full title (if relatively long).

> All groups develop fluid status hierarchies over time (Bourhis, "Status
>
> in Small Groups"). The gradual development of these status
>
> hierarchies have a profound effect upon role development (Bourhis,
>
> "Role Development in Small Groups") as well as the formation of
>
> normative behavior (Bourhis, "Norms").

M
L
A

PREPARING THE LIST OF WORKS CITED

The list of works cited appears at the end of the paper. Begin the list on a new page and number each page. Continue with the page numbers of the text. The title "Works Cited" appears centered at the top of the page. Double-space between the title and the first entry. Begin each entry flush with the left margin. If the entry runs more than one line in length, indent the second and each subsequent line of the entry five spaces from the left margin. Double-space the entire list, both between and within entries.

Arrange the entries in the list of works cited in alphabetical order by the author's last name. If the author's name is unknown, alphabetize the entry by the first word of the title other than "A," "An," and "The." For example: "The Recession is Coming" would be alphabetized under "R" in the list of works cited.

In citing two or more works by the same author in the works cited list, cite the author's name in the first entry only. Thereafter, use three hyphens (---) followed by a period, skip two spaces, and give the title.

Works Cited

Bourhis, John. "Classical Theory." Southwest Missouri State University, Springfield. 15 Sept. 1999.

---. "Systems Theory." Southwest Missouri State University, Springfield. 23 Oct. 1999.

DeVito, Joseph. The Interpersonal Communication Book. 6th ed. New York: Harper Collins Publishers, 1992.

Kramer, Michael, Ronda Callister, and Daniel Turban. "Information-Receiving and Information-Giving During Job Transitions." Western Journal of Communication, 59 (1995): 151-170.

M
L
A

CITING SOURCES OBTAINED ELECTRONICALLY

Increasingly, students and faculty are making use of electronic sources of information when conducting research. The days of "card catalogs" and wandering aimlessly through dusty library shelves looking for sources of information are over. Even the phrase "card catalog" may be meaningless for many contemporary writers. Current editions of the Modern Language Association and the American Psychological Association manuals do not include conventions for citing information obtained via the four most commonly used sources of electronic information: WWW pages, electronic collections, discussion lists, and electronic mail. Fortunately, suggested conventions for citing these forms of electronic material are available on-line. In particular, we suggest that you consult the MLA home page for updated conventions for all forms of citations, including electronic materials:

http://www.mla.org/main_stl.htm

The goal of any form of citation is to allow the information you have used in your manuscript to be retrieved again; either by you or someone else interested in your topic. Your citation must be complete and must allow someone else to retrace your steps in obtaining the information electronically. With electronic citations, it is especially important that punctuation and capitalization be accurate in the address. Use standard <u>MLA</u> rules and conventions for citing authors and sources discussed previously in this section, including rules for capitalization. The <u>MLA</u> home page provides the following guidelines for citing electronic material:

- Identify the name of the author, editor, compiler, or translator of the source (if available), reversed for alphabetizing and followed by any appropriate abbreviations (e.g., <u>Ed.</u>).
- Identify the title of the work whether it be a speech, poem, or article. If it is a posting from a discussion list, provide the title from the subject line in quotation marks followed by the descriptor "online posting." If the source is a web page, underline the title of the page or indicate some descriptor like <u>Home Page</u> if no title is provided.
- Provide the date of publication or of the last update if available. For discussion group postings or electronic mail, indicate the date of the message.
- Name the institution, sponsoring organization, or discussion group responsible for producing the source.
- Indicate the date that the material was accessed by the researcher.
- Provide a complete electronic address or URL of the source in angle brackets.

In general, these guidelines require electronic sources to follow the following format that can readily be adapted to various forms of electronic material:

Author's last name, first name. "Title of Specific Article, Web File,

or Online Posting." <u>Underline the Web Site Title</u> or use a

descriptor like Online Posting. Date of Publication or Revision.

Name of Sponsoring Institution. Date Accessed <Complete

Electronic Address>.

When using this format to cite electronic sources like web pages or electronic mail messages, minor adaptations are necessary. What follows are examples of commonly cited sources in proper MLA format.

M
L
A

WORLD WIDE WEB (WWW)

WWW pages usually provide all information necessary for correct <u>MLA</u> citation. In some cases, authors for a particular web page are not identified. The webmaster or system administrator of the web site may be viewed as the "editor" for that particular site. The following examples illustrate how various web pages should be cited.

Snyder, Alfred, Ed. "The Academy." <u>Debate Central</u>. University of Vermont.

5 May 1998 <http://debate.uvm.edu/academy.html>.

Young, Jeffrey. "U. Of Washington Tries a Soft Sell to Woo Professors to

Technology. <u>The Chronicle of Higher Education</u>. 28 May 1999. 1 June

1999 <http://www.chronicle.com/weekly/v45/i38/38a02301.htm>

ELECTRONIC COLLECTIONS

"AECT Publications." <u>Association for Educational Communications and</u>

<u>Technology Home Page</u>. 27 April 1998. Association for Educational

Communications and Technology. 5 May 1998

<http://204.252.76.75:80/Pubs/aectpubs.html>.

Oetting, Dan. "Eugene Debs: The Issue." <u>Douglass: Archives of American</u>
<u>Public Address</u>. 14 April 1998. Northwestern University. 5 May 1998
<http://douglass.speech.nwu.edu/debs_a80.htm>.

Trent, Judith. "An Invitation to Play a Role In NCA's Governance." <u>National</u>

<u>Communication Association Home Page</u>. 1998. National Communication

Association. 5 May 1998 <http://www.natcom.org/aboutNCA/leadership/

Invitation.html>.

CD ROM's

"Communication." <u>Microsoft Encarta 96 Encyclopedia</u>. 1995. Redmond,

   WA: Microsoft Corporation.

DISCUSSION LISTS

Driver, Dutch. "Applying Communication to COMGRADS." Online posting.

   12 May 1998. COMGRADS Hotline <COMGRADS@CIOS.org>.

Moreale, Sherry. "NCA Poster Session Task Force Report." Online posting.

   11 May 1998. CRTNET News <crtnet@natcom.org>.

ELECTRONIC MAIL (E-MAIL)

Olson, Loreen. "Worthwhile Competition." E-mail to the author. 27 April

   1998.

Titsworth, Scott. "Response to John Bourhis." E-mail to the author. 8 June

   1998.

CHAPTER TWO
A CONDENSED APA STYLE GUIDE

FORMATTING THE TEXT OF YOUR PAPER

TYPING

Unless otherwise instructed, all written work submitted for evaluation must be typed. The type must be clear, dark, and easily readable. Laser quality output has become the minimum acceptable standard for instructors as well as prospective employers. Use only standard typefaces such as Courier, Prestige Elite, Helvetica or Times Roman or their equivalents and standard type sizes (ten or twelve point). Only type on one side of the paper. Never use "fancy" or unusual fonts. Do not justify the right margin.

PAPER

Use only heavy white, 8½ by 11 inch bond paper. Never submit any work typed on erasable or "onion skin" paper. If you use erasable paper, have a high-quality photocopy made on heavy white, 8½ by 11 inch bond paper and submit the photocopy to your instructor. Keep the original copy for your files.

MARGINS

The newest edition of <u>APA</u> allows you to set your margins at either 1 inch or 1.5 inches top, bottom, left and right. Consult your instructor to see if she has a particular preference. Whichever size margins you choose, be consistent throughout the entire manuscript. Nothing should appear within the margins. Indent the first word of each paragraph five to seven spaces from the left margin. Quotations in excess of 40 words should be indented five spaces from the left margin, double-spaced, and without the usual paragraph indentation. Quotations in excess of 40 words and more than one paragraph in length should have the second and each additional paragraph indented five spaces from the new margin.

LINE SPACING

Your paper should be double-spaced throughout, including the heading, title, text, quotations, and references page.

A
P
A

Running head: MAGIC KINGDOM

Entering and Exiting the Magic Kingdom:

How Metaphors are used During the Organizational Assimilation

Process at Disney World

John S. Doe

Concordia College

A
P
A

CHAPTER TWO

TITLE PAGE

APA requires that your paper have a title page. The components of a title page are: the title of your paper, your name, institutional affiliation, and a running head. The title must also appear centered at the top of the first page of your paper followed by two spaces before the text of the paper begins. In APA, the preferred form of an author's name is first name, middle initial, and last name. Institutional affiliation refers to where the author(s) conducted the research. This includes your school. The running head is an abbreviated title that is printed at the top of the pages of a published manuscript to identify the article for readers. On your title page, type the running head in uppercase letters, flush left two lines below the pagination line. Beginning with the title, type the remaining information centered on the page, as shown in the example title page and in the sample papers in the appendixes.

PAGINATION

All scholarly writing requires pagination. Number all of the pages consecutively throughout the manuscript. Page "1" of the manuscript is the title page. Place all pagination in the upper right-hand corner, 1-1½ inches from the top and 1-1½ inches from the right of the page — depending on which margin size you have chosen. Remember, keep the margin area clear so your instructor has a place to make comments. To identify the manuscript, type the first two or three words from the title in the upper right-hand corner two spaces above the page number. Do not punctuate the page number in any way.

Magic Kingdom   1

A
P
A

BINDING

Unless otherwise instructed, neatly staple the pages of your paper together in the upper left hand corner. Do not tape, pin, or tear the corner(s) to bind the pages of your paper together. Unless specifically instructed to do so, do not submit your paper in a binder of any kind. Such bindings often make it difficult for instructors to easily grade your paper.

ABSTRACTS

<u>APA</u> requires an abstract for all papers/articles being submitted to a convention for presentation or journal for review and possible publication. Normally, this requirement is waived for the typical undergraduate paper. However, in special cases, your instructor may require that you write an abstract for your paper.

An abstract provides a comprehensive but brief (150-200 word) summary of the contents of a paper/article. The abstract should be descriptive of the contents of the work cited not evaluative. Do not indent the first word of the abstract.

An abstract for a theoretical article should contain the following information:
- a concise statement of the topic;
- a description of the purpose, thesis, or central construct that guides the work;
- the sources of information used in the book or article; and
- the conclusions and implications of the book or article as suggested by the author(s).

An abstract for an empirical study should contain the following information:
- the research question(s) or hypothesis(es) studied;
- a description of the subjects employed in the study including: number, type, age, sex, and selection procedures;
- a description of the experimental method(s) employed;
- the results of the study including significance levels where appropriate; and
- the conclusions and implications of the research as suggested by the author(s).

A
P
A

Abstract

A meta-analysis of 183 experiments comparing the effect sizes of

measurement techniques for assessing the effectiveness of public

speaking anxiety treatments was conducted. The comparison showed

differences between self-report, observer, and physiological

measurement techniques. However, no interaction was observed

between the type of therapy and the type of measurement technique.

The implications for measuring public speaking anxiety and the

classroom application of the results are considered.

From: Allen, M. (1989). A comparison of self-report, observer, and
physiological assessments of public speaking anxiety treatment
techniques using meta-analysis. Communication Studies, 40, 127-139.

A
P
A

SAMPLE APA ENTRIES

1.0 BOOKS

1.1 One Author

Northouse, P. (1997). Leadership: Theory and practice.

Thousand Oaks: SAGE Publications.

Kanter, R. (1977). <u>Men and women of the corporation.</u> New

York: Basic Books.

▲ *How do I know which words to capitalize in the title of a book?*

In book titles and subtitles, capitalize the first word of the title and of the subtitle, if any. Separate titles from subtitles with a colon. Include any other punctuation that is part of the title.

1.2 Two Authors

Deal, T., & Kennedy, A. (1982). <u>Corporate cultures: The</u>

<u>rites and rituals of corporate life.</u> Reading: Addison-Wesley.

Adler, R, & Marquardt, J. (1996). <u>Communicating at work:</u>

<u>Principles and practices for business and the professions</u> (5th ed.).

New York: McGraw-Hill.

1.3 Three or More Authors

Brilhart, J., Bourhis, J., Miley, B., & Berquist, C. (1992).

<u>Practical public speaking.</u> New York: Harper Collins.

Frey, L., Botan, C., Friedman, P., & Kreps, G. (1991).

<u>Investigating communication: An introduction to research</u>

<u>methods.</u> Englewood Cliffs, NJ: Prentice Hall.

1.4 Two or More Books by the Same Author

Bales, R. (1950). <u>Interaction process analysis: A Method for</u>

<u>the study of small groups.</u> Reading: Addison-Wesley.

Bales, R. (1970). <u>Personality and interpersonal behavior.</u>

New York: Holt, Rinehart and Winston.

1.5 Book with an Editor

Collins, R. (Ed.). (1985). <u>Three sociological traditions:</u>

<u>Selected readings.</u> New York: Oxford University Press.

1.6 Book with Two Editors

Knapp, M., & Miller, G. (Eds.). (1985). <u>Handbook of</u>

<u>interpersonal communication.</u> Beverly Hills: Sage.

Putnam, L., & Pacanowsky, M. (Eds.). (1983).

<u>Communication and organizations: An interpretive approach</u>.

Beverly Hills: Sage.

1.7 An Edition Other than the First

Babbie, E. (1997). <u>Survey research methods</u> (2nd ed.).

Belmont: Wadsworth Publishing Company.

Brilhart, J., & Galanes, G. (1995). <u>Effective group</u>

<u>discussion</u> (8th ed.). Dubuque: Wm. C. Brown.

1.8 A Work in a Book

Petronio, S., Bourhis, J., & Berquist, C. (1990). Families in

public places: But mom you promised! In J. DeVito & M. Hecht

(Eds.), <u>The nonverbal communication reader</u> (pp. 425-435).

Prospect Heights, IL: Waveland Press.

A
P
A

Redding, C. (1985). Stumbling toward identity: The

emergence of organizational communication as a field of study.

In R. McPhee & P. Tompkins (Eds.), Organizational

communication: Traditional themes and new directions (pp. 15-

54). Beverly Hills: Sage.

1.9 A Translation

Aristotle. (1954). The Rhetoric (W. R. Roberts, Trans.).

New York: Modern Library. (Originally published in 330 B.C.).

Cicero. (1954). Rhetorica ad Herennium (H. Caplan,

Trans.). Cambridge: Harvard University Press. (Originally

published circa 100 B.C.).

2.0 ARTICLES

The basic format for an article entry includes: author's name; date of
publication; title of article; name of periodical; volume number; and
page numbers.

2.1 One Author

Bingham, S. (1991). Communication strategies for managing

sexual harassment in organizations: Understanding message options

and their effects. Applied Communication Research, 19, 88-115.

Broome, B. (1991). Building shared meaning: Implications of a

relational approach to empathy for teaching intercultural

communication. Communication Education, 40, 235-249.

▲ *How do I know which words to capitalize in article and journal titles?*

Capitalize the first word of an article title and subtitle, if any. Separate a title from its subtitle with a colon.

Give the journal title in full. Capitalize all nouns, pronouns, adjectives, and adverbs. Do not capitalize coordinating conjunctions (and, but, for, nor, or) or prepositions introducing phrases (of, before, in, to). Do not capitalize an article (a, an, the) unless it is the first word of a journal title.

2.2 Two Authors

Hoffner, C., & Cantor, J. (1991). Factors affecting children's enjoyment of a frightening film sequence. Communication Education, 58, 41-62.

Petress, K., & King, A. (1990). Iran/Contra and the defeat of accountability. Communication Reports, 3, 15-21.

2.3 Three or More Authors

Buller, D., Strzyzewski, K., & Hunsaker, F. (1991). Interpersonal deception: I. deceivers' reactions to receivers' suspicions and probing. Communication Monographs, 58, 1-24.

Kreps, G., Frey, L., & O'Hair, D. (1991). Applied communication research: Scholarship that can make a difference. Applied Communication Research, 19, 71-87.

A
P
A

2.4 Monthly or Bimonthly Periodical

Fishman, K. (1991, June). Therapy for children. <u>Atlantic,</u>

pp. 47-81.

Erbe, B. (1999, June). Madame President? <u>Working Woman,</u>

p. 24

2.5 Weekly or Biweekly Periodical

Fineman, H., & Thomas, E. (1991, July 8). How far right?

<u>Newsweek,</u> pp. 19-20.

Cloud, J. (1999, May 31). Just a routine school shooting.

<u>Time,</u> pp. 34-43.

▲ *When citing an article in a periodical, when do I use quotation marks and when do I underline?*

Quotation marks are never used in <u>APA</u> unless they are part of the punctuation of a title. Do not underline article titles. Underline book and journal titles followed by a period. Underline the period following the book title. Underline the commas before and after volume numbers in a periodical citation.

3.0 NEWSPAPERS

The basic format for a newspaper entry includes: author's name; date; article title; name of newspaper; and page.

3.1 Signed Article from a Daily Newspaper

Mann, W. (1999, May 24). Mistakes in air war hurt NATO. The Kansas City Star, p. 1.

Bearak, B. (1999, May 23). Frozen in fury at the roof of the world. The New York Times, p. 1.

3.2 Unsigned Article from a Daily Newspaper

Reno should resign over spy scandal, senators say. (1999, May 24). USA Today, p. 1.

3.3 Signed Editorial from a Daily Newspaper

Squires, L. (1999, May 24). Don't be afraid of not knowing. Springfield News Leader, p. 6A.

Shapiro, W. (1999, May 24). Kosovo's plight is unbelievable yet undeniable. USA Today, p. 15A.

3.3 Unsigned Editorial from a Daily Newspaper

Airline tactics fair? (1999, May 24). Springfield News Leader, p. 7A.

Congressional term limit is the wrong answer. (1991, October 14). USA Today, p. 14.

4.0 UNPUBLISHED MANUSCRIPTS

Bourhis, J. (1998). Classrooms without walls: The future of Internet-based instruction. Unpublished manuscript.

5.0 UNPUBLISHED PAPERS PRESENTED AT MEETINGS

Stewart, C., & Adams, C. (1997, November) <u>Communication style,</u>

<u>leader-member exchange, and communication satisfaction.</u> Paper

presented at the annual meeting of the National Communication

Association, Chicago.

6.0 PERSONAL INTERVIEWS

The basic format for a personal interview includes: interviewee's name;
date; and the description: [Personal interview].

Berquist, C. (1999, January 25). [Personal interview].

Allen, M., & Tkachuk, H. (1999, February 1). [Personal interview].

7.0 LECTURES

The basic format for a lecture includes: lecturer's name; date; title of
lecture; and place where lecture was delivered.

Allen, M. (1999, September 1). Statistics for Dummies. University of

Wisconsin at Milwaukee. Milwaukee, WI.

Tkachuk, H. (1999, September 10). Losing Fishing Strategies for

Northern Pike. Concordia College. Moorhead, MN.

8.0 FILMS

The basic format for a film includes: director's name; date; film title;
[Film]; place of production; and studio.

Alda, A. (Director). (1981). <u>The four seasons</u> [Film]. Los Angeles:

Universal.

Hughes, J. (Director). (1985). The breakfast club [Film]. Los

Angeles: Universal.

9.0 TELEVISION PROGRAMS

The basic format for a television program includes: program title; date of broadcast; and network. If the television program was produced locally, include place of origin and station. Include the episode or segment title if readily available.

CBS evening news. (1991, October 25). CBS.

CNN headline news. (1992, January 16). CNN.

10.0 RADIO BROADCASTS

The basic format for a radio broadcast includes: program title; date of broadcast; and network. If the radio broadcast was produced locally, replace network with place of origin and station.

All things considered. (1991, October 24). National Public Radio.

Morning edition. (1992, January 2). National Public Radio.

A
P
A

CITING SOURCES IN THE TEXT OF YOUR PAPER

APA style uses parenthetical references for citing sources. Parenthetical references are placed within the text of the paper rather than at the bottom of each page (footnotes) or at the end of the paper (endnotes). The basic format for an APA parenthetical reference is: (author's last name, followed by a space, and the year in which the work was published).

For example:

Native English speakers tend to receive significantly higher scores on The

Speaking Proficiency English Assessment Kit (SPEAK) than non-native

English speakers (Powell, 1990).

▲ *When must I document a source?*

You must document a source whenever you:

1. directly quote, word-for-word, someone else's work;
2. paraphrase or summarize someone else's work; and/or
3. use facts and data that are not common knowledge.

As a way of adding variety to your citations, mention the author's name in the text and include the year parenthetically. For example:

Powell (1990) demonstrated that native English speakers tend to receive

significantly higher scores on The Speaking Proficiency English

Assessment Kit (SPEAK) than non-native English speakers.

When citing an entire work, the most elegant citation is to include the author (and possibly the work) in the text and include the year parenthetically.

In Thriving on Chaos: Handbook for a Management Revolution, Tom

Peters (1987) shatters many of the conventional myths regarding effective

management.

or

Peters (1987) shatters many of the conventional myths regarding effective

management.

When citing an English translation of a non-English work, include the author's name, the original date of publication, and the date of the English translation. For example:

The three primary forms of persuasion are *ethos*, *logos*, and *pathos*

(Aristotle, 330 B.C./1954).

When a reference contains a direct quotation, <u>APA</u> requires that a page number(s) be included in the parenthetical reference. The basic format for an <u>APA</u> parenthetical reference for a direct quotation is: (author's last name, space, date, space, "p." space, followed by the page number(s). For example:

"Culture plays a powerful role in human societies, especially in their

maintenance" (Casmir, 1991, p. 229).

The same rules apply when citing a direct quotation from a source with two authors. If the work cited has two authors, include the names of both authors each time the reference occurs in the text.

"No matter what they do or where they live, people in a highly developed

country spend much of their time in work groups, groups that are set up to

do a job" (Bormann & Bormann, 1988, p. 2).

▲ Notice that in the parenthetical reference the ampersand or "and" sign is used. In parenthetical references and in the list of references, <u>APA</u> uses the ampersand sign "&" instead of spelling the word "and" out. In the text of the paper, always use "and."

If the work cited has three or more authors, include the names of all authors the first time a reference is made to the work. In subsequent references, include only the first author's name followed by "et al." (meaning "and others"), followed by a space and the date.

First reference:

"It is our belief and the belief of perspective employers throughout the

United States that courses such as public speaking, listening, and

interpersonal communication should be included as an oral

communication core in such a blended program" (Curtis, Winsor, &

Stephens, 1989, p. 13).

Each subsequent reference:

> "From the results of this study, it appears that the skills most valued in the
>
> contemporary job-entry market are communication skills" (Curtis et al.,
>
> 1989, p. 13).

When a direct quotation exceeds forty words in length, <u>APA</u> requires that the quotation be "set-off" from the rest of the text. Introduce and cite the quotation as you would normally, omit the quotation marks, indent the entire quotation five spaces from the left margin, and write it in block form within the text. If the quotation exceeds forty words in length and contains more than one paragraph, indent the first word of each subsequent paragraph five spaces from the new left margin. For example:

> This particular study raises a number of issues that have heuristic value.
>
> > CA was originally conceptualized as the predisposition to experience
> >
> > anxiety when forced to communicate. The anxiety actually
> >
> > experienced during the communication event was not thought to
> >
> > affect the CA trait. In fact, reducing CA was discussed in terms of
> >
> > clinical treatment such as systematic desensitization. The results of
> >
> > the present study indicate that communication state anxiety
> >
> > experiences could reduce trait CA. (McCroskey, Beatty, Kearney, &
> >
> > Plax, 1985, pp. 181-182)

A
P
A

▲ *Note* that in the parenthetical reference "pp." is used to indicate that the quotation appears on more than one page of the cited material. Also note that in <u>APA</u> the concluding punctuation appears at the end of an extended quotation before the parenthetical reference. In <u>APA</u>, no punctuation follows the parenthetical reference for an extended quotation.

When citing a single work by an author of two or more works in the text of your paper, include the suffixes a, b, c, and so forth after the year.

All groups develop fluid status hierarchies over time (Bourhis,

1997c). The gradual development of these status hierarchies have a

profound effect upon role development (Bourhis, 1997b) as well as

the formation of normative behavior (Bourhis, 1997a).

PREPARING THE LIST OF REFERENCES

The list of references appears at the end of the paper. Begin the list on a new page and number each page. Continue with the page numbers of the text. The title "References" appears centered at the top of the page. The title "Reference" is used if there is only one reference in the paper. Double-space between the title and the first entry. Begin each entry indented five spaces from the left margin. If the entry runs more than one line in length, the second and each subsequent line should be flush left. Double-space the entire list, both between and within entries.

Arrange the entries in the list of references in alphabetical order by the author's last name. If the author's name is unknown, alphabetize the entry by the first word of the title other than "A," "An," and "The." "The Recession is Coming" would be alphabetized under "R" in the list of references. When ordering several entries by the same author, arrange the entries chronologically from earliest to latest. When ordering entries with the same first author and different second authors, arrange the entries alphabetically by second author. Single author entries precede multiple-author entries beginning with the same surname:

A
P
A

References

McCroskey, J. (1985).

McCroskey, J., & Richmond, V. (1987).

When listing multiple works by the same author with the same date of publication, arrange your entries on the reference page alphabetically by title ignoring "a, and, the" when they appear as the first word in a title.

References

Bourhis, J. (1997a, March 17). Norms. Southwest Missouri State University, Springfield, MO.

Bourhis, J. (1997b, March 12). Role development in small groups. Southwest Missouri State University. Springfield, MO.

Bourhis, J. (1997c, March 10). Status in small groups. Southwest Missouri State University. Springfield, MO.

CITING SOURCES OBTAINED ELECTRONICALLY

Increasingly, students and faculty are making use of electronic sources of information when conducting research. The days of "card catalogs" and wandering aimlessly through dusty library shelves looking for sources of information are over. Even the phrase "card catalog" may be meaningless for many contemporary writers. Current editions of the Modern Language Association and the American Psychological Association manuals do not include conventions for citing information obtained via the four most commonly used sources of electronic information: WWW pages, electronic collections, discussion lists, and electronic mail. The most recent edition of the APA Manual uses Li and Crane's format for citing electronic citations. A summary of their suggestions may be found on-line at the following address:

http://www.uvm.edu/~ncrane/estyles/espub.html

The goal of any form of citation is to allow the information you have used in your manuscript to be retrieved again; either by you or someone else interested in your topic. Your citation must be complete and must allow someone else to retrace your steps in obtaining the information electronically. With electronic citations, it is especially important that punctuation and capitalization be accurate in the address. Use standard <u>APA</u> rules and conventions for citing authors and sources discussed previously in this section, including rules for capitalization. Although there are no accepted <u>APA</u> conventions for citing electronic works, here are some suggestions based on Li and Crane's work:

- Identify the name of the author, editor, compiler, or translator of the source (if available), reversed for alphabetizing and followed by an abbreviation (i.e., Ed.) if appropriate.
- Provide the date of publication or of the last update if available. For discussion group postings or electronic mail, indicate the date of the message. This date should be enclosed in parentheses. If no date is available, indicate "No date" in parentheses.
- Identify the title of the work whether it be a speech, web page, or article. If it is a posting from a discussion list or electronic mail, provide the title from the subject line.
- Provide the name of the web site, discussion group, or other electronic source you are referencing. This title should be underlined.
- Brackets containing a description of the electronic medium (e.g., Online, CD-ROM, etc.) should follow the title of the web site, discussion list, or CD ROM you are referencing.
- Name the institution, sponsoring organization, or discussion group responsible for producing the source.
- Provide a complete electronic address, URL, or other information about availability including any commands necessary for retrieval from a server.
- In brackets, indicate the date that the material was accessed by the researcher.

In general, these guidelines require electronic sources to follow the following format that can be readily adapted to various forms of electronic material:

Author's last name, first initial. (Date of publication, revision, or indicate no date). Title of specific article. In <u>Name of Web Site or Electronic Source</u> [medium]. Name of Sponsoring Institution. Available: complete electronic address and other information about availability [access date].

When using this format to cite electronic sources like web pages or electronic mail messages, minor adaptations are necessary. What follows are examples of commonly cited sources in proper APA format.

WORLD WIDE WEB (WWW)

WWW pages usually provide all information necessary for correct APA citation. In some cases, authors for a particular web page are not identified. The webmaster or system administrator of the web site may be viewed as the "editor" for that particular site. The following examples illustrate how various web pages should be cited.

Snyder, A. (Ed.). (No date). The Academy. In Debate Central [On-line].

University of Vermont. Available: http://debate.uvm.edu/academy.html

[1998, May 12].

Soukup, C. & Titsworth, S. (1998, May 1). The Toulmin Project Home

Page. In COMM109 Home Page [On-line]. Department of Communication

Studies, University of Nebraska. Available:

http://www.unl.edu/speech/Toulmin [1998, May 11].

ELECTRONIC COLLECTIONS

AECT Publications. (1988, April 27). In Association for Educational

Communications and Technology Home Page [On-line]. Association for

Educational Communications and Technology. Available:

http://204.252.76.75:80/Pubs/aectpubs.html [1988, May 5].

Oetting, D. (1988, April 14). Eugene Debs: The issue. In Douglass:

Archives of American Public Address [On-line]. Northwestern University.

Available: http://douglass.speech.nwu.edu/debs_a80.htm [1988, April 14].

Trent, J. (1988). An Invitation to Play a Role In NCA's Governance. In

National Communication Association Home Page [On-line]. National

Communication Association. Available:

http://www.natcom.org/aboutNCA/leadership/Invitation.html [1988, May 5].

CD ROM's

Communication. (1995). Microsoft Encarta 96 Encyclopedia [CD

ROM]. Available: Redmond, WA: Microsoft Corporation.

DISCUSSION LISTS

When citing discussion lists the availability information should include any
necessary commands required to retrieve the message from the discussion
listserv. For example, the listserv at the University of Pittsburgh allows access
to archives of the CRTNET discussion group by using the "index" command.
If such a command is not provided, the "help" command may be used to get
information on how to access archives. The following examples illustrate how
these commands may be included in citations.

Driver, D. (1988, May 12). Applying communication to COMGRADS.

COMGRADS Hotline [On-line]. Discussion group posting. Available E-

Mail: LISTSERV@CIOS.org/help [1988, May 12].

Moreale, S. (1988, May 11). NCA poster session task force report.

CRTNET News [On-line]. Available E-Mail: LISTSERV@lists.psu.edu/index

[1998, May 11].

A
P
A

ELECTRONIC MAIL (E-MAIL)

Olson, L. (olson@server.edu). (1998, April 27). Worthwhile essay competition (fwd). E-mail to Scott Titsworth (scott@server.edu).

Levine, T. (tl@server.edu). (1998, February 5). 1-tailed F's. E-mail to Scott Titsworth (scott@server.edu).

A
P
A

CHAPTER THREE
SPECIALIZED WRITING ASSIGNMENTS

In academic writing, some assignments require that you follow standard guidelines for particular types of writing. Among these are annotated bibliographies, research abstracts, research critiques, reviews of literature, and research reports.

COMPOSING AN ANNOTATED BIBLIOGRAPHY

An annotated bibliography is a list of sources of information on a specific topic which includes a short summary of the content of each of the works listed. Your instructor may establish specific criteria for topics and work selections. Annotated bibliographies can be written using either the MLA or APA condensed style guides. Each entry in an annotated bibliography provides the reader with two essential pieces of information about the work cited: how to locate the work (source citation) and a brief summary of the contents of the book, book chapter, or journal article (abstract).

CITING SOURCES

In composing an annotated bibliography, follow the rules for citing sources of information in a works cited page (MLA) or references (APA).

THE ABSTRACT

Abstracts can be either brief or extended. Consult with your instructor for any specific instructions regarding the content of an abstract. An extended abstract provides a comprehensive but brief (150 - 400 word) summary of the contents of a book or article. A brief abstract capsulizes the source's content in 100 - 150 words. Brief and extended abstracts should be descriptive of the contents of the work cited, not evaluative. Indent the entire abstract five spaces from the left margin.

SAMPLE BRIEF ABSTRACT ENTRY

Williams, D. (1984). 2001: A Space Odyssey: A warning before its time. Critical Studies in Mass Communication, 1, 311-322.

In this article, Williams demonstrates how Kenneth Burke's concepts of hierarchy and the redemptive process can be used to analyze and interpret a film rhetorically. Williams suggests that 2001: A Space Odyssey was a warning to the human species to avoid becoming overly dependent on technology and that the ending of the film offered a religious vision to transcend this technological dependence.

An extended abstract for a book or theoretical article should contain the following information:

- a concise statement of the topic;
- a description of the purpose, thesis, or central construct that guides the work;
- the sources of information used in the book or article; and
- the conclusions and implications of the book or article as suggested by the author(s).

An extended abstract for an empirical study should contain the following information:

- a description of the purpose of the study;
- the research question(s) or hypothesis(es) studied;
- a description of the subjects employed in the study including: number, type, age, sex, and selection procedures;
- a description of the method(s) employed;
- the results of the study including significance levels where appropriate; and
- the conclusions and implications of the research as suggested by the authors. (See Appendix C for a sample extended abstract.)

COMPOSING A RESEARCH CRITIQUE

A critique of a research article contains all the elements of an extended abstract plus a detailed criticism or evaluation of the work cited. Instructors often limit the works you may select to reports of original empirical or humanistic research in the field of Speech Communication. You may also be required to submit a photocopy of the article you have selected along with your critique. A research critique can be written using either the MLA or APA condensed style guides. See Chapter 4 for a representative list of scholarly journals which may contain reports of original empirical or humanistic research. A sample research critique is provided in Appendix D.

CITING SOURCES

In composing a research critique, follow the rules for citing sources of information in a works cited (MLA) or references page (APA).

THE CRITIQUE

A critique of a research article provides important information about an empirical or humanistic research article in two parts: (1) a summary of the article (abstract) and (2) a critique of the article. A typical research critique will average between 1,000 to 1,500 words in length.

In the summary (abstract) of an original empirical or humanistic study include the following information:

- a brief statement of the purpose and rationale of the study;
- the research question(s) or hypothesis(es) studied;
- a description of the subjects employed in the study including: number, type, age, sex, and selection procedures;
- a description of the method(s) employed, including the content of surveys, questionnaires, and interviews and the procedures used to collect the data;
- the results of the study including significance levels where appropriate; and
- the conclusions and implications of the research as suggested by the authors.

Your instructor may provide you with specific criteria to use in evaluating original empirical or humanistic studies. An excellent resource for reading and evaluating communication research is <u>Interpreting Communication Research: A Case Study Approach</u> by Frey, L.R., Botan, C.H., Friedman, P.G., and Kreps, G.L. (1992, Prentice Hall). Absent specific instructions, apply the following criteria in critiquing original research:

- ***theoretical scope***: Does the study apply to a broad domain of the communication process? How might we extend the knowledge provided by the study to other contexts?
- ***appropriateness of methodology***: Are the study's methodology and reporting of results appropriate for answering the proposed research question(s) and/or hypothesis(es)?
- ***validity***: Does the study satisfy the requirements for external and internal validity? Do the authors provide an adequate/interesting explanation of the data? Were the hypotheses clearly tested? Are the results of the study generalizable? Are there other plausible explanations for the results other than those offered by the researcher?
- ***heuristic value***: Does the study's methodology, results, and conclusions help to generate future research? Are the conclusions non-obvious?
- ***parsimony***: Relative to other studies, does this study provide the simplest, most logical explanation of the area being studied? Was the design of the study only as complicated as it needed to be to test the hypothesis(es) or research question(s)?

COMPOSING A REVIEW OF LITERATURE

A review of literature is a summary of previous research relative to a given topic or question. A review of literature should give the reader a clear overview of what is known about the topic, including summaries of research conclusions, various methods used to investigate the topic, and indications of what areas remain to be investigated. A review of literature differs from an annotated bibliography by providing more than separate summaries of the sources included. Reviews of literature point out common themes in existing research and draw conclusions about the "state of the art" regarding knowledge in the given area. Researchers generally conduct and write a review of literature prior to proposing a specific research project in order to determine what important questions remain to be explored and to provide a rationale for their specific study.

A review of literature is a common writing assignment, one that may serve as the culmination of a course or the first step in a larger research project. Your instructor may give you specific instructions regarding the length of your review of literature and the scope of sources which must be included. A review of literature might range from a paper of a few pages to a dissertation chapter of more than 100 pages. In composing a review of literature, follow the guidelines of either the MLA or APA condensed style guides, including a works cited (MLA) or references (APA) page. See Appendix E for an excerpt from a review of literature.

Here is a common format for a review of literature:

- *Introduction*: Introduce the topic and provide a preview of what is to follow in the paper.
- *Problem Statement*: Briefly describe the significance of the research you are reviewing and/or the importance of conducting such a review. For example, you might argue that significant gaps exist in the research to date, that research findings have been inconsistent, or that different bodies of research need to be integrated for an improved understanding of a topic or research problem.
- *Review*: The review is more than just a string of individual abstracts. It is a thorough review organized around a specific thesis. The problem statement should provide clear focus for the review. Clear and smooth transitions between main points are especially important. The reader should be guided to a clear conclusion by the information and arguments presented in the review. In a review of literature, some sources may be treated in great detail, while others are mentioned only briefly as examples or supporting evidence.
- *Conclusion*: Restate the thesis of your paper and summarize key points. Indicate the implications of the review, such as any new research questions, applications of existing research, or integration of diverse sources.

COMPOSING A RESEARCH REPORT

A research report provides the reader with specific information about a piece of original, empirical research that the author has conducted. You are in essence "reporting" the design and results of your research project to a larger community. A research report follows the same general format found in journal articles reporting original empirical or humanistic research. The length of a research report will vary depending on the complexity of the study, the space devoted to reviewing past research, and to the nature of the data being reported. Research reports may be prepared following either the <u>MLA</u> or <u>APA</u> condensed style guides. Your instructor may give you specific guidelines to follow, but most research reports follow a standard format.

- a statement of the purpose of the research, often stated in terms of a "research problem" that needs to be addressed;
- a review of past research (review of literature) relevant to the research topic, demonstrating the author's understanding of the area and building a rationale for the present study;
- a statement of the study's hypothesis(es) and/or research question(s), justified on the basis of the review of literature;
- a description of the methods employed in the study: for empirical studies, a description of the study's participants, data-gathering methods, procedures, and evidence of the reliability and validity of measures and procedures; for humanistic studies, a description of the criteria used in selecting texts or events for analysis and a description of the theoretical or methodological approach taken;
- a summary of the study's results, including specific answers for each of the research question(s) and/or hypothesis(es); and
- a discussion of the implications of the results, explanations for the results, limitations of the research, and suggestions for future research in the topic area.

CHAPTER THREE

CHAPTER FOUR
LOCATING SOURCES OF
COMMUNICATION RESEARCH

Many writing assignments require you to locate and read primary source material, including reports of original research, critical reviews of past research, and theoretical essays. In addition to book-length publications, most primary source material is found in scholarly journals. This chapter provides information about journals that publish communication research, indexes you can use to search for information on specific topics, and Internet resources for investigating the communication discipline.

SCHOLARLY JOURNALS IN COMMUNICATION

Scholarly journals are very different from popular magazines (such as Time or Newsweek) and trade publications (such as Advertising Age or Communication World). One important difference is that scholarly journals are read primarily by scholars and professionals, as opposed to the general public or people with only a casual interest in the subject matter. A second important characteristic of scholarly journals is that they are more specialized than most popular periodicals. Scholarly journals often are dedicated to a particular discipline (such as communication or psychology), and may even be dedicated to particular areas of a discipline (for example, health communication or nonverbal communication). Finally, popular periodicals and trade publications do not typically publish full-length reports of original research, whereas scholarly journals exist as an outlet for researchers and theorists to publish their original works.

Below are descriptions of selected scholarly journals which publish reports of original empirical and humanistic research, including their Library of Congress call numbers. (At the end of this chapter you'll find a more complete list of communication-related journals which you may want to consult in doing your research.) Note that some journals are considered "national" or "international" journals by virtue of their being published by national or international associations or having national and international circulations. Other journals are considered "regional" journals since they are published by regional associations, such as the Central States Communication Association, although many regional journals have national circulations. The journals described below are national or international unless otherwise identified.

- Communication Education is published quarterly in January, April, July, and October by the Speech Communication Association (PN 4071 S73). Communication Education publishes scholarly articles regarding communication in instructional settings. Articles in Communication Education focus primarily on the role of communication in the instructional process and teaching communication in traditional academic environments and non-traditional settings (e.g., business, health, and legal settings). Manuscripts submitted to Communication Education must conform to the guidelines set forth in the Publication Manual of the American Psychological Association (4th ed.) and may not exceed 30 pages. Manuscripts submitted as brief reports should not exceed 14 pages. Communication Education is indexed in Communication Abstracts and Index to Journals in Communication Studies, among other indexes.

- Communication Monographs is published quarterly in March, June, September and December by the Speech Communication Association (PN 4077 S6). Communication Monographs publishes articles dealing with communication in a wide variety of contexts, with most articles reporting original research grounded in theory. Submissions must conform to the guidelines set forth in the Publication Manual of the American Psychological Association (4th ed.) and should not exceed 30 pages (approximately 9,000 words). Communication Monographs is indexed in several sources, including Communication Abstracts, Index to Journals in Communication Studies, Psychological Abstracts, and Sociological Abstracts.

- Communication Quarterly is published quarterly (Winter, Spring, Summer and Fall) by the Eastern Communication Association and thus is considered a regional journal (PN 4071 T6). Manuscripts appearing in Communication Quarterly include research reports, critical studies, state of the art reviews, and critical essays. Submissions must conform to either the Publication Manual of the American Psychological Association (4th ed.) or the MLA Style Manual (1985). Communication Quarterly is indexed in Communication Abstracts and the Index to Journals in Communication Studies.

- Communication Reports is published in the Fall, Winter, Spring, and Summer (P91.3 .c66). It is a scholarly academic journal that publishes short (2500 words or less) data-based articles on a wide variety of topics related to the field of communication as broadly defined. Authors are expected to devote a significant portion of the manuscript to the reporting and analysis of research data. Manuscripts that are primarily theoretical or speculative in nature are not appropriate for this journal. Manuscripts must conform to the guidelines set forth in the Publication Manual of the American Psychological Association (4th ed.). Communication Reports is a publication of the Western Speech Communication Association and is therefore considered a regional journal in the field. Communication Reports is indexed in Communication Abstracts, Sociological Abstracts, PSYCHINFO, and Social Planning/Policy and Development Abstracts.

- Communication Research is published bi-monthly in February, April, June, August, October, and December, by Sage Publications, Inc (P91 C56). Articles in Communication Research usually report results of empirical studies. The journal emphasizes the development and testing of communication theory that cuts across contextual boundaries (e.g., organizational communication, interpersonal communication). Manuscripts which report purely applied research without clear grounding in theory are not appropriate for this journal. Submissions to Communication Research must conform to the guidelines set forth in the Publication Manual of the American Psychological Association (4th ed.). Communication Research is indexed in a variety of sources, including, Index to Journals in Communication Studies, ERIC/EAC, Expanded Academic Index, Human Resources Abstracts, Index to Journals in Mass Communication, Psychological Abstracts, Sociological Abstracts, and Social Science Citation Index.

- Communication Studies is published quarterly in the Spring, Summer, Fall and Winter by the Central States Communication Association and is considered a regional journal (PN 4071 C4). Articles published in Communication Studies reflect a diversity of topics and approaches, including rhetorical/humanistic scholarship as well as empirical research. Manuscripts must conform to the guidelines set forth in the Publication Manual of the American Psychological Association (4th ed.). Communication Studies is indexed in several sources, including Communication Abstracts and Index to Journals in Communication Studies.

- Communication Theory is published quarterly and is a scholarly journal sponsored by the International Communication Association (P87 .c66x). Manuscripts in this journal are expected to address specific issues of theory development, evaluation, and criticism. As such, many articles are critical essays rather than research reports. Manuscripts must conform to the guidelines set forth in the Publication Manual of the American Psychological Association (4th ed.). Communication Theory is indexed in Communication Abstracts and Index to Journals in Communication Studies, among other indexes.

- Critical Studies in Mass Communication is published quarterly in March, June, September, and December by the Speech Communication Association (P87 C7). CSMC provides an academic forum for interpretive approaches to mass communication theory and research. Approaches represented in the journal include critical philosophy, political economy, rhetorical and media criticism, literary theory and semiotics, feminist scholarship, cultural studies, and pragmatism. Articles may report original research, critically review past research, or develop new theoretical ideas and directions. Manuscripts must conform to the guidelines set forth in the Publication Manual of the American Psychological Association (4th ed.) and should not exceed 30 pages. CSMC is indexed in Communication Abstracts and Index to Journals in Communication Studies, among other indexes.

- Health Communication is a quarterly journal devoted to the publication of scholarly research on the relationship between communication processes and health (P87 .H43x). Topics range from interpersonal (e.g., physician-patient interaction) to mass media (e.g., effects of health education campaigns) and encompass a variety of research methods and approaches. Manuscripts must conform to the guidelines set forth in the Publication Manual of the American Psychological Association (4th ed.). Health Communication is indexed in Communication Abstracts and other indexes.

- Human Communication Research is published quarterly in September, December, March, and June by the International Communication Association (P91.3 H85). It is a scholarly academic journal and the majority of articles published in Human Communication Research reflect a behavioral and social scientific approach. Articles in this journal may report original research, methodological issues, critical reviews of existing research, as well as theoretical and philosophical essays on the study of communication. Manuscripts must conform to the guidelines set forth in the Publication Manual of the American Psychological Association (4th ed.). Human Communication Research is indexed in several sources, including Communication Abstracts, Index to Journals in Communication Studies, Social Sciences Citation Index, Psychological Abstracts, and Sociological Abstracts.

- The Journal of Applied Communication Research is published in February, May, August and November (HM258 .J67) . As its title suggests, this journal emphasizes the publication of articles that address relationships between actual "practice" and theories of communication, criticism, rhetoric and/or performance. Authors are expected to apply field specific "theory" in an effort to solve clearly defined social problems or clarify contemporary social issues in a wide variety of contexts. Manuscripts cannot exceed 25 pages in length and must conform to guidelines set forth in the Publication Manual of the American Psychological Association (4th ed.). The Journal of Applied Communication Research is a publication of the Speech Communication Association, and it is indexed in both the Index to Journals in Communication Studies and Communication Abstracts.

- The Journal of Broadcasting and Electronic Media (PN 1991 J6)is published quarterly in February, May, August, and November by the Broadcast Education Association. As its title suggests, this journal publishes a wide variety of research in the fields of broadcasting and electronic media, including studies on media effects, audience behavior, and media technology. Contents of this journal are indexed in a number of sources, including Arts & Humanities Citation Index, Communication Abstracts, Current Contents, Current Index to Journals in Education, Index to Journals in Communication Studies, Psychological Abstracts, and Sociological Abstracts.

- The Journal of Communication is published quarterly by the International Communication Association (P 90 J6). Articles span a wide variety of topics, while a majority of the articles address questions related to media, culture, and policy. This journal emphasizes research cross-disciplinary research. The editors recommend that manuscripts not exceed 30 pages and require that they conform to the guidelines set forth in the Publication Manual of the American Psychological Association (4th ed.). The Journal of Communication is indexed in several sources, including, Communication Abstracts, Index to Journals in Communication Studies, ERIC Current Index to Journals in Education, Film Literature Index, International Index to Television Periodicals, Psychological Abstracts, and Sociological Abstracts.

- The Quarterly Journal of Speech is published quarterly in February, May, August, and November by the Speech Communication Association (PN 4071 Q3). The Quarterly Journal of Speech primarily publishes humanistic scholarship in rhetorical studies and rhetorical criticism. Submissions must conform to current guidelines of either the American Psychological Association or the Modern Language Association and should not exceed 8,000 words in length. Contents of the Quarterly Journal of Speech are indexed in Education Index, Index to Journals in Communication Studies, and Sociological Abstracts.

- The Southern Communication Journal is published quarterly (Fall, Winter, Spring and Summer) by the Southern States Communication Association (PN 4071 S65). Articles from all theoretical and methodological traditions are welcome, although the journal historically has been dominated by rhetorical scholarship. Manuscripts must conform to the guidelines set forth in the Publication Manual of the American Psychological Association (4th ed.) and must not exceed 6,000 words (approximately 25 pages). The Southern Communication Journal is indexed in Communication Abstracts and the Index to Journals in Communication Studies.

- Text and Performance Quarterly is published quarterly by the National Communication Association (PN2 T498). Articles in TPQ cover a broad range of communication topics relating to personal, social, and cultural performances. Authors are expected to explore performance as it relates to a variety of social phenomena. A variety of methodologies may be employed including critical, ethnographic, and rhetorical. Manuscripts must conform to the guidelines established by the Modern Language Association and should not exceed 9000 words. Articles appearing in TPQ are indexed in Communication Abstracts and Index to Journals in Communication Studies, among other indexes.

- The Western Journal of Communication is published quarterly by the Western States Communication Association and is considered a regional journal (PN 4071 W45). The journal publishes articles in a variety of communication areas, including rhetorical criticism, interpersonal communication, philosophy of communication, organizational communication, and free speech. Manuscripts should conform to either The MLA Style Manual (1985) or the Publication Manual of the American Psychological Association (4th ed.). Western Journal of Communication is indexed in Communication Abstracts and in the Index to Journals in Communication Studies.

USING INDEXES TO LOCATE SOURCES IN COMMUNICATION

Scholarly journals are indexed and abstracted in a wide variety of publications and computerized data bases. Many of these resources index journals across a wide variety of disciplines. For example, Social Sciences Index and Humanities Index will help you find material from many different fields. Most communication journals are included in these broad-based indexes. In addition, there are several indexes which are devoted entirely to communication studies, and these may be particularly useful to you if you are new to reading primary resource material in communication. The two most prominent communication indexes are Communication Abstracts and Index to Journals in Communication Studies Through 1990. A detailed description of these two indexes is provided here, followed by brief descriptions of several other indexes and resources you may find useful in conducting your research.

- Communication Abstracts: This index is published bi-monthly (February, April, June, August, October & December) and provides brief summaries, or abstracts, of the most recently published articles, books, and reviews related to communication, including speech communication, media, journalism, film, and other related areas. The last issue of each year contains cumulative author and subject indexes for that year. Also, issue #5 (October) includes a complete list of all publications that are abstracted in that year's volume. There are three ways to use Communication Abstracts:

  1. Browse through the abstract entries until you find an article that appears interesting or relevant to you, then locate the article using the source citation given there.

  2. Use the subject index in the back of each issue to locate abstracts of publications on specific topics, then locate the article using the source citation.

  3. Use the author index in the back of each issue to locate articles by a specific researcher.

The subject and author indexes in Communication Abstracts are easy to use. Next to each subject or author entry appears one or more numbers. The numbers correspond with the numbered abstracts in that issue. For example, next to the topic "persuasion" you might find the numbers 251, 263, and 285.

This tells you there are three sources abstracted in that issue related to "persuasion." Simply locate the three abstracts by their numbers.

Each abstract contains several pieces of useful information. First, a complete bibliographic citation is provided so that you may locate the original source. Second, an abstract of approximately 150 words describes the purpose and contents of the source, including methods and results for research reports. Finally, a list of key terms by which the source is indexed is provided. For example, if one of the articles you found on "persuasion" was a study on the effectiveness of television commercials, key terms might include: advertising, brand recall, commercials, consumer behavior, perception, and television. You then could use these key terms to search for additional sources related to your specific topic.

- Index to Journals in Communication Studies Through 1990. This index is updated every several years and is published by the Speech Communication Association. It is also referred to as the Matlon Index, after its editor, Ronald J. Matlon. The Index to Journals in Communication Studies Through 1990 (IJCS) references nineteen journals, including, Quarterly Journal of Speech, Communication Monographs, Communication Education, Critical Studies in Mass Communication, Southern Communication Journal, Western Journal of Speech Communication, Communication Studies, Communication Quarterly, Association for Communication Administration Bulletin, Philosophy and Rhetoric, Journal of Communication, Human Communication Research, Journalism Quarterly, Journal of Broadcasting and Electronic Media, Argumentation and Advocacy, Text and Performance Quarterly, Communication Research, Journal of Applied Communication Research, and Women's Studies in Communication. A new expanded CD-ROM version of this index, CommSearch, is also now available (see below).

The IJCS is divided into three parts. Part I gives the title of every article in every issue of each journal from its first issue through 1990. Publication dates and volume numbers are shown for each issue. Each publication has a letter code (e.g., M = Communication Monographs). An identifying number is shown to the left of each article, with the publication code letter being the first character.

Part II is the Index to Contributors. For each author, articles are listed by their identifying numbers. Find the identifying number in Part I to locate the title of the article and its precise reference.

Part III is the Index of Subjects. There are six broad headings, including "Communication," "Education," "Business," and "Fine Arts." Under each heading are listings which give the identifying numbers of each article in that area. There is also a key word index of subjects that allows you to quickly locate a group of listings on a particular topic.

Here is an example of how you might use the IJCS to locate an article on deceptive communication written by Steven A. McCornack and Timothy R. Levine. If you knew the author(s), but not the exact citation, you would use Part II: Index to Contributors. Under McCornack, Steven A. (p. 542) you would find several coded entries, including M1355, M1361, and H385. Look up each of these entries in Part I: Table of Contents. M1361 would take you to the section for Communication Mongraphs (p. 93), where you would find the full citation for the article, "When Lovers Become Leery: The Relationship Between Suspicion and Accuracy in Detecting Deception." You would then use the bibliographic information to locate the article in the library's collection of Communication Monographs.

Suppose you did not know of any specific articles on deception, but were using the index to locate articles on the topic. Using Part III: Index to Subjects, you would look under the keyword "deception" (p. 738) and find 38 coded entries, representing 38 different articles related to deception, including M1361, which refers you back to the same article by McCornack & Levine.

Unlike Communication Abstracts, the Index to Journals in Communication Studies does not provide summaries of the indexed articles. However, the great advantage of IJCS is its immediate access to every article ever published in each of the nineteen journals.

In addition to these two paper resources, there are two computerized databases devoted specifically to the communication discipline with which you should become familiar: CommSearch and ComIndex. Contained on CD-ROM and diskette, respectively, these resources are held by many libraries and also are available to individuals at reasonable prices.

- CommSearch, a CD-ROM database of journals focusing on the discipline of communication. CommSearch is produced by the National Communication Association. CommSearch includes all of the information contained in the Index to Journals in Communication Studies plus several additional features. First, CommSearch includes information through 1995. Second, CommSearch allows you to search abstracts from the six NCA journals. Third, CommSearch includes the full texts for articles in the six NCA journals for 1991 through 1995, with future editions to expand to include earlier years.

- ComIndex: An Electronic Index to the Literature of the Communication Discipline, is an author and title index published by the Communication Institute for Online Scholarship. It is available on diskette for IBM PC or compatible personal computers. ComIndex references 60 international journals and annuals from the field of communication. The database can be searched by authors' names or by words in article titles. Other features include the ability to narrow your search to specific years and even to specific journals. A brief description of each journal in the index also is included in this program.

Communication research is indexed in a variety of other sources, including indexes of scholarship in other disciplines related to communication. Here is a brief listing of printed and computerized indexes that you may find useful.

- Business Education Index (1940 —), indexes materials related to business.
- Business Periodicals Index (1958 —), indexes all categories of business journals.
- Communication Abstracts (1991 —), see above.
- Current Contents: Social and Behavioral Sciences (1974 —), reproduces tables of contents for 1300 journals and articles from edited books.
- Current Index to Journals in Education (1969 —), indexes contents of education journals.
- Dissertation Abstracts (1966 —), abstracts doctoral dissertations in the United States and Canada.
- ERIC (1966 —), is a CD-ROM index combining the Current Index to Journals in Education and Resources in Education. Many unpublished papers presented at academic and professional conferences are available through ERIC.
- Humanities Index (1974 —), indexes over 340 English-language periodicals in the humanities.
- Index to Journals in Communication Studies (1974, — 85, — 90), see above.
- IAC Business Index (1990 —) , indexes over 900 journals and business newspapers with citations concentrated in the field of business.
- IAC Expanded Academic Index (1990 —), indexes over 1500 journals, including many in communication as well as other social sciences and humanities.
- PAIS Bulletin (1915 — 1990), indexes books, periodicals, and documents on contemporary public issues. Continued as PAIS International in Print.

- <u>Psychological Abstracts</u> (1927 —), indexes and abstracts sources related to the field of psychology.
- <u>Psyclit</u> (1974 —), is a CD-ROM version of Psychological Abstracts.
- <u>Resources in Education</u> (<u>RIE</u>) (1966 —), indexes research in education, most of which is not published elsewhere.
- <u>Social Sciences Index</u> (1974 —), indexes over 350 English-language periodicals related to the social sciences.
- <u>Sociological Abstracts</u> (1953 —), indexes and abstracts sources related to the discipline of sociology.
- <u>Sociofile</u> (1974 —), is a CD-ROM version of Sociological Abstracts.

SEARCHING, SURFING, AND BROWSING: USING ON-LINE RESOURCES

Indexes are useful for locating published sources on particular topics, but there are even more timely ways of keeping up-to-date on the latest developments in various fields. A large variety of on-line bulletin boards, LISTSERV user groups, web sites, and electronic publications are available to you via computer. By accessing these sources you can "listen in" on current debates among scholars and experts — or even participate yourself! You can also locate information and resources not available anywhere in print. Below is a brief listing of several on-line sources you may find helpful and interesting. There are many more, and more are being added every day. Most sites on the world wide web also have built-in "links" to other related sites. Following these links is an easy way to explore sites related to your interests.

American Communication Association: The ACA is a national organization of communication scholars and professionals from across the discipline. Its web site includes extensive resources, including bibliographies, interest groups, an index of on-line books and texts, and a wide array of links to related sites. Contact the ACA web site at <http://www.americancomm.org/>

Applied and Organizational Communication Network: This is a LISTSERV discussion group with participants primarily from the fields of management and communication (app-orgcom@creighton.edu; subscribe by sending a message to <u>majordomo@creighton.edu</u>).

Center for Electronic Texts in the Humanities: This web site includes an inventory of electronic texts in the humanities, including more than 75 journals, and access to collections of electronic texts <http://www.ceth.rutgers.edu>

Communication Research and Theory Network (CRTNET): CRTNET is a LISTSERV discussion group maintained by the National Communication Association. Participants post notices ranging from discussions of theoretical and practical issues to announcements of conferences. Transcripts of major political speeches, such as the President's State of the Union Address or presidential campaign speeches, are also routinely posted on CRTNET. Participation in CRTNET is free. To subscribe, send the following message to the LISTSERV (listserv@psuvm.psu.edu): subscribe crtnet your first and last names. Then on a separate line type the word, quit.

Comserve: This is an on-line service of the Communication Institute for Online Scholarship. Comserve provides access to a resource library of scholarly papers, research materials, bibliographies, syllabi, archives of online discussions, and newsletters, as well as interest group "hotlines" and The Electronic Journal of Communication/La Revue Electronique de Communication. Some of Comserve's services are free, while others are reserved for those who pay an individual membership fee or departments that are institutional affiliates. Two particularly useful member services are ComAbstracts, a database of abstracts in the professional literature, and ComWebMegaSearch, a full text index of over 12,000 publication titles in the field of communication. For more information about Comserve, send an e-mail message to Comserve@cios.org. There is also a Comserve web site <http://www.cios.org>

International Communication Association: ICA, a major international association for academics and professionals in many areas of communication, maintains this web site. Available here are information about ICA, listings of conference programs, bibliographies, and links to other related sites <http://www.icahdq.org/>

Scholarly Journals Distributed Via the World Wide Web: This site maintained by the University of Houston Libraries provides information about on-line scholarly journals in a variety of disciplines http://info.lib.uh.edu/wj/webjour.htm

National Communication Association (formerly Speech Communication Association): The national office of NCA, one of the major associations for academics and professionals in the field of communication, maintains a web site that includes information about upcoming conferences, NCA members, and even job placement <http://www.nation.org/>

Uncover Reveal: This unique service will automatically e-mail you the table of contents of a large variety of scholarly journals. Contact Uncover Reveal by sending a Telnet message to database.carl.org and following the instructions.

A REPRESENTATIVE LIST OF
SCHOLARLY COMMUNICATION JOURNALS

American Speech
Argument Studies Quarterly
Association for Communication Administration Bulletin
Broadcasting
Cinema Journal
Communication
Communication and the Law
Communication and Cognition
Communication Education
Communication Monographs
Communication Quarterly
Communication Research: An International Quarterly
Communication Research Reports
Communication Studies
Communication Theory
Communication Yearbook
Critical Studies in Mass Communication
Educational Communication and Technology
European Journal of Communication
Film Comment
Film Journal
Health Communication Research
Human Communication Research
Information and Behavior
International Journal of Advertising
International Journal of American Linguistics
Journal of Applied Communication Research
Journal of Broadcasting and Electronic Media

Journal of Communication
Journal of Language and Social Interaction
Journal of Popular Film
Journalism Quarterly
Language
Language and Communication
Language and Social Psychology
Language and Speech
Linguistics
Management Communication Quarterly
Marketing and Media Decisions
Mass Communication Review
Media and Methods
Media and Values
Media Culture and Society
National Forensic Journal
Philosophy and Rhetoric
Political Communication and Persuasion
Quarterly Journal of Speech
Quarterly Review of Film Studies
Rhetoric Society Quarterly
Southern Communication Journal
Telecommunication Journal
Text and Performance Quarterly
Western Journal of Speech Communication
Women's Studies in Communication
World Communication

CHAPTER FIVE
CHOOSING SUPPORTING MATERIAL WISELY

Previous chapters focused on the conventions for proper formatting and citation in scholarly writing. Although strict adherence to such conventions is necessary for effective writing, authors must make other decisions affecting the quality of a manuscript. For instance, how does one decide whether to use one piece of supporting material rather than another? Are some sources better to use than others? Are Internet and WWW sources appropriate for scholarly writing? Will readers be more persuaded by some sources but not by others? These are only a few of the many questions authors must consider when selecting supporting material for a research paper, essay, or speech.

This chapter moves away from the objective conventions of formatting and citation to discuss *subjective* decisions made by authors that can dramatically impact the quality of a manuscript. Specifically, we identify several guidelines or "rules of thumb," for selecting and using support material. We begin with a discussion of why it is necessary to critically evaluate sources before including them in a manuscript. Next, we identify nine guidelines for evaluating support material and then apply them to several Internet sources relating to the topic of gender communication. Finally, we identify common errors related to the use of supporting material that we have encountered in student research papers, essays, and speeches.

THE NECESSITY FOR SOURCE EVALUATION

Contemporary writers are faced with a double-edged sword created by the exponential growth of information. Although the amount of available information in every academic discipline has dramatically increased, not all sources of information are equally reliable and appropriate for use in scholarly writing. Although it is easier to find supporting material, it is much more difficult to determine what supporting materials should be included in a well developed manuscript.

Essays, research projects and even speeches are argumentative in nature. The goal of the manuscript or speech outline is to develop a well-reasoned argument for some stated conclusion. For that reason, supporting material may be viewed as building blocks for the author's argument. Authors must make subjective decisions concerning the use of supporting material so that their arguments make the strongest possible case for their conclusion. More specifically, writers are justified in critically evaluating sources for two reasons: First, there is a pragmatic necessity to limit the amount of supporting material included in a scholarly project. Second, there is an ethical responsibility to only include supporting material that is accurate and appropriate. We expand on both of these justifications and include examples illustrating the necessity of source evaluation.

THE PRAGMATICS OF SOURCE EVALUATION

Anyone using the Internet to conduct research has encountered frustration when searching for a specific source using one of the popular search engines like Webcrawler or Yahoo. These search tools return hundreds or thousands of possible sources and the researcher is left with the options of painstakingly viewing each source, randomly checking sources that look remotely relevant, or simply giving up. Unfortunately, the researcher's difficulty does not end there. For any given topic there may be hundreds of research articles, books, government documents, and popular press articles that could also be relevant. Thus, the researcher is faced with the overwhelming task of sifting through a seemingly endless list of possible references. Because of time constraints and length limitations, one cannot possibly review and include every possible source on a given topic.

To illustrate the pragmatic necessity of source evaluation, we used Webcrawler to search for sources related to a literature review on computer assisted instruction (CAI). In this example, a total of 198,112 Internet sources matched the search criteria! Armed with too much information, what steps might be necessary to make our list of sources more manageable?

The first step is to recognize that all two-hundred thousand sources cannot be reviewed for inclusion in a manuscript. If for no other reason than time, the list of possible sources must be reduced to a reasonable number that can receive more detailed attention. How many sources should receive systematic review? The answer to this question can vary greatly depending on the specific circumstance (i.e., the length of the writing assignment). For this example, we may want to limit our search to the first 25 sources returned by the search engine.

Even after our search list has been limited in scope, the subjective decision-making process has not ended. Do we include all 25 sources in our literature review or do we select a few of those sources and expand on them in greater detail? Again, the answer to this question can vary depending on the nature of the writing assignment. For instance, a typical literature review may reference several of the very best sources and explain a few of them in detail while other projects may survey many of the available sources. Regardless of the specific nature of the writing assignment, however, it should be clear that the author must be selective when evaluating supporting material. Specifically, there are two lessons that should be learned from the above example: First, the writer must reduce the number of possible sources and then decide which of those sources should be included in the assignment. Second, pragmatic decisions about the use of supporting material in a manuscript are almost always dictated by the nature of the writing assignment (i.e., how much time you have to gather and review material, how long your manuscript or outline can be, etc.).

THE ETHICS OF SOURCE EVALUATION

Although there is a strong pragmatic rationale for evaluating sources, there are also compelling ethical reasons why an author must be selective about the use of supporting material. Ethical decision-making can revolve around several issues related to the use of supporting material. For instance, should the writer include counter-viewpoints or only present material supporting his or her argument? Is it ethical to include sources that may only be marginally qualified? Is it ethical to include a source that may be biased? Should the writer include secondary sources that have not been verified? These and other ethical questions are faced by writers whenever they engage in the writing process.

Writers and speakers alike are reminded that they have an ethical obligation to their audience. In our opinion, this is the single most important guideline that guides research. The author of a speech or manuscript acts as a gatekeeper who presents a filtered view of information to the audience and, in many cases, the audience will base their understanding of the information on what the author presents. For that reason, the author must ensure that the audience can make an informed decision about the information presented. The guidelines we present in the next section were selected because they are based, in part, on the author's ethical responsibility to the audience.

SIX GENERAL GUIDELINES FOR EVALUATING SOURCES

When researching a topic it is often necessary to develop a "screening" process for supporting material. For instance, the previous example of CAI sources on the Internet illustrates the need to quickly sift through many potential sources to find sources most relevant to the issue being addressed. In this section we present several general guidelines that authors may use to screen potential sources for possible inclusion in a speech or manuscript. These guidelines are most useful in early stages of research when one is trying to compile a working list of sources directly applicable to the topic in question.

1. Is the supporting material clear?

Supporting material may be used for a variety of purposes in a manuscript or speech; not the least of which is to add clarity to arguments being presented. In some cases, supporting material is used to define important concepts or terms. For instance, the model paper contained in appendix A uses a variety of different sources to clarify and define "culture" for the reader. In other cases, supporting material is used to clarify and support essential claims. The same paper uses supporting material to support the author's judgements of culture at Southwest Airlines. If supporting material is to accomplish any of these purposes it must be clear to the reader or listener. Without clarity, supporting material may confuse rather than strengthen arguments.

How can authors evaluate the clarity of supporting material? One technique is for authors to determine whether or not the supporting material needs additional explanation before audience members or readers will understand its connection to the argument being made. For instance, does the supporting material use technical jargon not easily understood without further explanation? Are the implications of statistical findings articulated by the source, or will you have to provide additional explanation? Does the material require a certain level of background knowledge before understanding is possible? For any given piece of supporting material it may be necessary to provide adequate explanation before the relevance of the source is clear. In such circumstances, the author must question whether the material is worth including if a great deal of additional explanation is necessary. There may be other sources providing clearer explanations of the term or concept and, in such circumstances, those sources may be a better alternative.

2. Is the supporting material consistent?

Consistency questions whether a particular source is consistent with other sources on the same topic (external consistency) and also whether the source is consistent with itself (internal consistency). In terms of external consistency, authors should determine whether a particular source presents the same conclusion as other sources on the same topic. If the source in question takes a contrary position from the majority of other sources, the author must determine which of the possible conclusions are best supported.

Several research areas in communication provide examples of external *inconsistency*. Suppose a group of researchers conducted several experiments testing whether or not courses in public speaking increase students' communication competence. Even if public speaking courses do increase students' levels of communication competence we could expect that, because of chance, each study may find slightly different results and as many as one out of five such experiments may find no statistically significant effects. If you were writing a literature review on these experiments how could you reconcile such inconsistency?

Regardless of whether you are reviewing statistically-based research reports, qualitative studies, or critical analyses of discourse you must determine which conclusions carry more weight either because of theoretical support, strong methodology, or consistency with other research findings. For instance, one may choose to cite studies having larger sample sizes when reconciling inconsistency among statistical findings since larger sample sizes can reduce the influences of chance on statistical results. Alternatively, one may decide to use a particular research finding because it is consistent with several other findings or is justified on theoretical grounds. In short, authors should determine whether or not the supporting material they intend to use is consistent with other sources on the same topic. When sources are not consistent, authors should attempt to reconcile that inconsistency and use findings that appear most valid.

A second concern related to consistency is whether or not supporting material is internally consistent. Does the source in question present the same line of reasoning throughout or are there contradictions present? Are conclusions found in the source supported through well developed arguments or empirical data? Does the source of the supporting material draw similar conclusions in other articles, books or electronic documents? Obviously, it is unwise to include supporting material wrought with contradictions. Such contradictions can not only harm the credibility of that particular source, but they can also harm the credibility of your manuscript.

3. Is the supporting material verifiable?

Recall that the primary function of correct source citation, whether it be in APA or MLA style, is to aid readers who are interested in finding additional information or verifying the sources used in the manuscript. Thus, a third guideline for evaluating the usefulness of supporting material is the extent to which the material is verifiable.

When grading various writing assignments and public speeches we have often encountered students using personal interviews with roommates, friends, and even "people on the street" as supporting material. Although these sources can, in some cases, help make topics more concrete for audience members or readers, theses sources are often difficult to verify. The same problem can occur when using personal e-mail and even WWW documents. Since web pages can be updated several times a day it may be impossible to verify what was on a particular web page when the initial research was gathered. Authors are encouraged to avoid using unverifiable supporting material when making important claims in their manuscripts or speeches. If using such evidence for anecdotal purposes, additional evidence from verifiable sources is warranted.

4. Is the source of the supporting material competent?

Source qualification is an often overlooked component of supporting material. Put simply, source competence assumes the source of the supporting material has some experience or expertise with the topic in question. Without such qualifications, the conclusions drawn from a source may amount to nothing more than uneducated guesswork.

Whether or not a source is competent can depend on the type of supporting material and the function it is serving in the manuscript or speech. For instance, examples and personal testimony are often used to illustrate concepts but they rarely come from highly qualified sources. Other instances involving definitions or technical explanations may require more qualified sources. When evaluating the qualifications of sources, one should attempt to answer the following questions: Does the source have significant experience with the topic in question? Is the source considered an authority in the field? Has the source conducted original research on the topic? Is the source well respected? Obviously, the goal is to include the most qualified sources for a given topic.

5. Is the source of the supporting material unbiased?

Related to the competence of the source is the question of whether or not the source is biased or predisposed to take a certain position on the topic in question. Consider the current national debate regarding violence in schools. On this particular issue, a researcher should be skeptical of supporting material obtained from the National Rifle Association. Clearly, this organization and its representatives have a very strong motive for advocating a particular viewpoint on this issue.

Although bias is self-evident on a controversial topic like gun control, writers must be aware that biases can exist on any given issue: A researcher may have a bias toward a particular theoretical perspective or research methodology; a book author may have a bias toward a particular political ideology; even a friend may have a bias influencing their viewpoint on an issue. When using any source it is important to question whether individual biases cloud their judgement on an issue to such a degree that their conclusions are not sound. Moreover, authors have an ethical responsibility to point out potential biases when presenting supporting material to readers and audience members.

6. Is the supporting material relevant?

The final general guideline questions whether or not supporting material is relevant to the topic in question. It seems self-evident that one should not include "irrelevant" supporting material, however, students often perceive an advantage to using the "shotgun" approach for researching a topic. That is, instead of focusing research efforts on key arguments supporting the claim of the manuscript inexperienced writers often include supporting material that only tangentially relates to the issue being addressed. Although this strategy can give the appearance of a well documented speech or paper, careful readers and listeners can see through this strategy. As a general rule, it is wise to include a few quality sources and explain those sources well rather than including several sources that are minimally explained and have little relevance to the specific issue being addressed.

In summary, writers and speakers have an ethical responsibility to insure that the supporting material they use is accurate, objective and relevant to their topics. When choosing between various supporting material, ask yourself the following six questions:

1. Is the supporting material clear?
2. Is the supporting material consistent?
3. Is the supporting material verifiable?
4. Is the source of the supporting material competent?
5. Is the source of the supporting material unbiased?
6. Is the supporting material relevant?

SPECIFIC GUIDELINES FOR EXAMPLES, TESTIMONY AND STATISTICS

When researching a speech or research paper authors often have specific objectives in mind. For instance, a literature review on communication apprehension may need to include a definition of the concept, a synthesis of research exploring the concept, and some examples illustrating its debilitating effects. Even with these specific objectives in mind, it is often difficult to determine what example(s) to include, which statistics are most valid, or what sources are most qualified. This section presents several questions authors may use to evaluate the quality of three common types of supporting material: Examples, testimony, and statistics. These questions may be considered in conjunction with the general guidelines described previously.

1. Questions to consider when using examples.

As a form of supporting material, examples are primarily used for their rhetorical force in explaining arguments. Because examples are useful for illustrating concepts, facts, theories, relationships and other points being made in a manuscript or speech, they have the effect of making ideas concrete for listeners and readers. To ensure that examples are accomplishing their illustrative function, authors should analyze whether particular examples are typical and representative of other possible examples illustrating the same idea.

First, examples should be typical of other examples illustrating the same idea. Whether or not an example is typical questions the extent to which it is similar or dissimilar to other examples. Highly similar examples are more typical whereas atypical examples deviate from other examples in some substantive way. Consider for instance a qualitative research project intended to develop a grounded theory of anticipatory socialization into organizations. The researcher may interview several individuals who are preparing to enter an organization for the first time to draw conclusions about communication processes essential for effective socialization. When reporting the results of the study, the researcher will likely use examples from the interviews to capture the essence of the emergent theory. How would the study be affected if the researcher relied on examples containing markedly different descriptions of the socialization process? Would such examples be useful when describing the grounded theory? Would the researcher be more justified in using similar examples to illustrate a particular concept? Obviously, the success of the study depends on finding typical examples to develop conclusions about the nature of communication in anticipatory socialization. Using atypical examples may heighten awareness of limitations to the grounded theory but would serve little utility for explaining the theory. This same principle may be applied to nearly every situation where examples are used. Put simply, examples are more effective for illustrating a concept if they are similar to other examples.

The second test for using examples considers whether or not they are representative. Recall that the primary function of examples is to illustrate real-world instances of some concept being discussed. The question of representativeness assumes that particular examples should be sufficiently broad in scope to *fully* illustrate the concept. Are important elements of the concept included in the example? Is the example applicable to a wide range of situations and experiences? Are there other examples providing a more complete illustration of the concept? Examples that are limited in their applicability may leave readers and listeners confused about the general nature of the concept being discussed. Thus, when writing a speech or paper, authors should find examples that fully illustrate the concept in question and can be applied to a wide range of situations.

2. Questions to consider when using testimony.

Using testimony involves statements from other sources to support claims made in a manuscript or speech. In general, testimony can either be from an expert in the field or a layperson who has experienced the concept being discussed. Lay testimony should be treated like an example and evaluated accordingly. However, expert testimony requires a separate set of questions to evaluate its effectiveness as supporting material.

The key question for expert testimony centers on the qualifications of the source being used. Good use of testimony requires sources who are respected as accomplished experts in the field. Moreover, those qualifications may need to be articulated if the audience or readers are not familiar with the source. For instance, most audiences will not be familiar with sources quoted in a speech and, in such cases, the speaker must identify the qualifications of the source to get maximum rhetorical impact from the evidence. The speaker may explain qualifications by identifying the source's title (i.e., Chief Executive Officer, Congressional Representative, Senior Researcher, etc.), awards (i.e., Nobel Prize Winner), or research (i.e., the number of books, articles, or research studies the source has published on the topic). By explaining these qualifications the source will appear more credible to the audience and, in turn, will improve the speaker's credibility.

Although the importance of source credibility is clear for public speeches, these same principles do not necessarily apply to instances of scholarly writing. When constructing a literature review on nonverbal communication, would it be necessary or appropriate to indicate the qualifications of each source cited in the review? Fortunately, writers of research papers are not required to place the same emphasis on identifying source qualifications as are speakers. Because manuscripts have bibliographies, readers can easily investigate the qualifications of particular sources if they so wish. However, the fact that a manuscript may not contain descriptions of source qualifications does not absolve authors from recognizing the importance of this criterion. For any given research topic there are likely seminal books and articles that should be cited when explaining the concept. For instance, almost every literature review and scholarly article on communication apprehension cites James McCroskey's definition of the concept. Indeed, one may question the legitimacy of a manuscript that does not cite "classic" works in the area being addressed. This example illustrates a principle for using testimony in a manuscript: When engaging in scholarly writing projects, effective use of testimony depends less on actual qualifications and more on the readers' recognition of the source's contribution to knowledge on the topic in question. How does one determine what constitutes a classic or seminal work? The most obvious strategy is to determine who other researchers cite. For example, one would only need to read a handful of articles on dramatism to recognize that Kenneth Burke, Erving Goffman and Ernest Borman are key sources associated with that particular theoretical perspective.

3. Questions to consider when using statistics.

Numerous books and academic journals are devoted to the issue of statistical validity and, therefore, a complete description of the concept is beyond the scope of this book. There are, however, general evaluative principles that may be applied to statistics by any researcher regardless of mathematical expertise. The guidelines for evaluating statistics differ depending on whether the statistics are descriptive or inferential in nature. We define both types of statistics and provide specific questions assessing their validity as supporting material.

Descriptive statistics provide quantitative descriptions of an entire population's characteristics. Census data, the gross national product (GNP), and demographic breakdowns of students at a particular university are examples of descriptive statistics. Notice that these examples involve statistics representing the characteristics of nearly everyone or everything contained in the population being studied. The example of a school's demographic data may involve analysis of every student's record to determine age, gender, ethnic background, hometown, etc. Likewise, the GNP is a statistic representing the aggregate dollar amount of all materials produced by a country for a particular year.

When evaluating descriptive statistics, two questions should be addressed. First, do the statistics actually represent the entire population? For instance, a common criticism of census data is that some individuals (e.g., people who are homeless) may slip through the data collection process. If the number of people not included in data collection is sufficiently large, the derived statistics may not be valid descriptors of the population. A second question to consider for descriptive statistics is whether or not the source responsible for compiling the statistics is trustworthy. Unfortunately, statistics are easy to fabricate or distort and, consequently, descriptive statistics are only useful when they come from a respected source.

Unlike descriptive statistics, inferential statistics draw conclusions about a population based on data collected from a select sample. Most generally, researchers use random sampling techniques to collect data and form conclusions about an entire population. For instance, political pollsters for a presidential election cannot possibly contact every single voter to project election results. Instead, a random sample of a few thousand people may be used to make projections.

When evaluating inferential statistics, authors should first determine whether or not the sample used in a study allows for valid conclusions to be drawn. To determine the validity of a sample, one may consider the sample size, the demographic composition of the sample, whether or not the sample was truly random and whether or not the sample is typical and representative of the population (see the section on examples for an explanation of typicality and representativeness). For instance, many researchers in communication use samples drawn from college students to form conclusions about communication phenomena. Can researchers draw valid conclusions about topics such as doctor-patient communication or superior-subordinate communication using a sample of college students who may lack significant experiences in these areas? Can one form conclusions about the nature of romantic relationships by only surveying college students? An important question of validity for inferential statistics involves the sample used in the study. Most research articles contain a description of the sample used and authors should carefully assess such information before relying on statistical results to form conclusions.

There are other guidelines for evaluating inferential statistics that should be addressed. Although it is not possible to explain each, we do highlight several principles that one may consider. We encourage authors who are inexperienced with statistics to consult faculty members or other resources for additional explanation.

- Generally, larger sample sizes in proportion to the population allow for more powerful results.
- Inappropriate use of statistical procedures can increase the likelihood of chance results.
- Statistical significance does not prove the truth or falsehood of something.
- A "statistically significant" finding does not necessarily make something "meaningfully significant." Statistical findings are only meaningful when supported with strong theoretical explanations.
- Statistics are only snapshots of reality. Their validity and meaning can change in time or across samples.
- Only specific research designs allow conclusions about causal relationships.

APPLYING EVALUATION GUIDELINES TO INTERNET SOURCES

The Internet is rapidly changing the way research is conducted. In our opinion, students are too dependent on supporting material gained from the WWW. Although the trend toward using the Internet as a primary research tool is not surprising, it is alarming. Our position is direct: many WWW sources are of poor quality and consequently are inappropriate for use in formal academic writing, whether it be a speech outline or research paper. In addition, students are not being adequately trained to make meaningful distinctions between sources of supporting material that are credible and appropriate versus those that are deceptive, unreliable and potentially harmful to others.

As discussed earlier, the advantage offered by the WWW is often counteracted when writers do not discriminate among sources. Put simply, not all sources of information are good and effective writers must learn steps necessary for distinguishing among sources quickly. This section illustrates how several of the guidelines may be applied to WWW sources. We pay particular attention to the issue of source credibility and qualifications and explain steps necessary for determining the source of WWW pages.

For this example we conducted an Internet search for information on gender communication. We begin with a description of how we used a search engine to find possible sources on the Internet. We then describe several steps taken to evaluate the quality of those sources.

USING SEARCH ENGINES WISELY

Understanding how to conduct searches on the Internet using several of the popular search engines like Webcrawler, InfoSeek, or Hotbot can facilitate more efficient research attempts. For this example we used the phrase "Gender and Communication" as our search term. Most search engines also allow connecting terms (e.g., "and," "or," "not") to be placed between separate search terms. In some cases, using such connectives can filter irrelevant sites from search results. Most search tools on the Internet provide a help page containing tips for advanced searching techniques. By following these tips, the precision of searches can be dramatically increased.

Using Webcrawler, we found 755 web pages containing both "gender" and "communication." Percentages were returned indicating the statistical match with the search request. For this example, we chose to highlight only four of the returned sites to illustrate how one might apply some of the guidelines mentioned in the previous section. These descriptions are exactly as they appeared in the search results.

- Gender and Sexuality (66%)
  This page publishes texts which address gender studies and queer studies, with a particular focus upon discussions of sex, gender, sexual identity and sexuality in cultural practices.
  http://english-www.hss.cmu.edu/gender/

- NAGDT Home Page (66%)
  Are you looking for resources and answers to gender diversity issues in the workplace? Annual conference open to all individuals, businesses and organizations. http://www.gendertraining.com/

- PROceedings: Browse Papers Division 31 (65%)
  Pippa Norris, Harvard University Gender and Political Communication II
  Gender, Elections and Public Opinion I: US Feminism and Political
  Community. http://pro.harvard.edu/panels/31/D31.htm

- CMC Magazine March 1996 (64%)
  Please visit our sponsor: Advertising Info Computer-Mediated
  Communication Magazine, ISSN 1076-027X / Volume 3, Number 3 /
  March 1, 1996. Lisa Schmeiser introduces this special issue on women
  and gender online...
  http://www.december.com/cmc/mag/1996/mar/toc.html

Results for this search include a title for the web site and additional
information including a brief description of the site, the statistical match with
the search request, and the Internet address. Most search engines include an
option to return summaries and other information with search results, however,
this option may need to be selected. By obtaining summaries and addresses
for the web sites, researchers can quickly determine the relevance of each site
to their research project.

EVALUATING THE SOURCE OF INTERNET MATERIAL

As one becomes more familiar with conducting research on the WWW it is
easier to explore search results quickly. More importantly, experience using
the WWW can help researchers become more effective at screening potential
information to find the very best sources available on a topic. For instance,
experienced WWW users can quickly distinguish between the quality of web
sites by examining the format of a web page, how often the web page has been
accessed, and whether or not there are grammatical and spelling errors present
on the page.

Several strategies may be used by researchers when assessing the quality of
Internet sources. Just by examining summaries of web sites, researchers can
quickly assess the quality of possible sources in terms of how relevant they are
to the topic in question. For instance, we may quickly dismiss the second
source from our example list since it is a private corporation's web page and
not a scholarly source. Although it is often easy to recognize WWW pages
created by private organizations, notice how the brief description of the second
source leaves the impression that this web page describes a conference on

gender in the workplace. In fact, this source is an advertisement for a profit-making training program. For a mere $1,200 one may be able to attend the workshop and learn more information! Basic knowledge of Internet addresses can help researchers determine what type of organization created the Internet site and consequently avoid wasting time reviewing sources like the NAGDT Home Page. In general, Internet addresses follow this format:

Protocol://document-type.server.suffix/directory/file.name

The protocol and document type are typically the "Http://" and "WWW" designations. The server is simply the name of the actual computer where the WWW page is located. In particular, researchers should pay attention to the suffix of the web site. There are four possible suffixes: .edu (education), .org (organization), .com (commercial), .gov (government), and .net (network). For our example, two of the sources come from education servers (the site titled "Gender and Sexuality" and the site titled "PROceedings: Browse Papers Division 31"), and two came from commercial servers ("NAGDT Home Page" and "CMC Magazine March 1996"). The Internet address may also contain an additional suffix if the server is from a country other than the United States. For instance, a document housed on an Australian server has the suffix ".au" after the primary suffix.

How can the Internet address be used to apply general guidelines for evaluating sources? Although this is a gross generalization, education servers and government servers may be more relevant for academic research than commercial and network servers. Organization servers may be appropriate for use if the organization is a recognizable not-for-profit organization like the American Red Cross or the National Communication Association. Researchers should understand that Internet addresses can be obtained easily, and consequently, they should not be used as the only indicator of a particular source's quality. For instance, most students and faculty can easily obtain university accounts and publish web pages with an ".edu" suffix, however, those web pages may not be reliable for academic research. Moreover, the CMC web page in our search results provides popular press articles on gender issues in computer mediated communication. Thus, even though the CMC site is from a commercial (i.e., ".com") server, it would be appropriate for review.

Once sites are selected for possible inclusion in a manuscript or speech, what other information might a researcher need to obtain before determining whether or not to use a particular source? Initially, authors should review each site to determine whether or not a source is identified, when the last time the site was updated, and what the purpose of the site is. In some cases, it may be necessary to backtrack and find the index page for a particular site to obtain this information. For instance, the returned address for the PROceedings page is for a particular file and not the main page for that website. To find out relevant information about this site, it is necessary to view the actual index page (usually, one can find the index page by clicking a "return to home page" link in a particular web file). Once this information is obtained, the researcher can determine the credibility and biases of the source. In our example of the PROceedings page, we were able to determine that this website reported research presented at the 1998 meeting of the American Political Science Association – a source which is relevant for our project.

Once all of this information has been reviewed, researchers should evaluate the ideas contained in a web document as if it were a journal article, book, or magazine. In particular, the researcher may apply several of the guidelines described previously. In light of the possible evidence for a particular issue, do the web pages clearly explain and illustrate the concept? Are the web pages internally and externally consistent? Is it possible to verify conclusions drawn by the sources? In particular, we stress the fact that information obtained via the WWW must be verifiable. Recall that verification requires that sources and arguments can be confirmed. To apply this principle, we adhere to the *independent confirmation standard.* The independent confirmation standard simply requires that before using any material, one should first find other sources making the same claims, observations, or drawing the same conclusions. By obtaining independent confirmation, one is fulfilling ethical responsibilities toward the audience by ensuring that information contained in a manuscript or speech is accurate. For our topic of gender communication, we might seek independent confirmation by consulting volumes of Women's Studies in Communication or one of the several textbooks on this issue before using any WWW material. Effective researchers make use of a variety of different sources of supporting material, including traditional resources found in a library.

FINAL THOUGHTS ON CHOOSING SUPPORTING MATERIAL WISELY

In this chapter we have provided several suggestions for researching and evaluating support material. After reviewing this information, it should be clear that good research involves much more than simply compiling a list of sources. Good research involves systematic evaluation of sources to find the best possible supporting material for arguments being made in a manuscript or speech.

Although a valuable research tool, the Internet compounds many of the problems faced by contemporary researchers. Sources from the Internet often lack the precision, qualifications, and rigor necessary for support material in scholarly writing. Authors have both ethical and pragmatic reasons for evaluating Internet sources carefully. In particular, authors should adhere to the standard of independent confirmation before relying on any material obtained from the WWW.

To aid authors in evaluating all types of supporting material, we outlined several guidelines for determining the quality, reliability, and effectiveness of supporting material. These guidelines may be used to quickly sort through potential sources and can also be used to evaluate specific forms of supporting material present in those sources.

Although the guidelines articulated in this chapter are quite useful for evaluating sources, they do not guarantee a mistake-free manuscript or speech. To conclude, we offer several suggestions for using support material wisely. These suggestions should be considered when revising and putting final touches on a research paper or speech outline.

- Internet addresses for web sites should not be cited as the "source" of a web site. They are address not sources. Instead, the author, editor, webmaster, or sponsoring organization should be cited as the "source." The Internet address is analogous to the title of a journal and therefore would only be included in the bibliography. It would be like providing the address for your school library as the "source" of supporting material in your paper! Imagine how silly you would sound, "According to 901 South National Avenue in Springfield, Missouri . . . ."

- If you cannot identify the source of the supporting material you have found on the WWW do not use it in a scholarly paper or speech. You have no way of accessing the quality of the supporting material you have found absent this information. Try to verify the supporting material you have found from another source, either on the WWW or preferably in print, and use that source instead. If you cannot identify the source of your supporting material it is the equivalent of using an anonymous source, which is considered to be inappropriate for scholarly purposes.

- Many Internet sources are dubious in terms of quality. Before using any material obtained from the WWW, authors should independently confirm the material to ensure accuracy, preferably from a printed source available in your library.

- Different types of support material accomplish different functions in a manuscript or speech. In most cases, it is necessary to use a variety of types of support material so that all of these functions are fulfilled. Avoid the temptation to rely too heavily on supporting material obtained from the WWW because it is convenient to do so. The essence of good speaking and variety is variation in source material. Just as you should not rely solely on supporting material found in newspapers, so to should you not use material found only on the WWW.

- Support material should be balanced in a speech, essay, or research paper. For instance, each main point in a speech must include enough supporting material to adequately support the specific issues being addressed in the point.

- WWW sources of supporting material that have printed equivalents are no better or worse than their printed equivalent. For example, The New York Times on the web is no more or less credible than The New York Times in print. The National Rifle Association's printed newsletter is no better or worse then the electronic version of the NRA's newsletter. A source that is incompetent remains incompetent whether in print or on the WWW.

- We always recommend to our students to print a hard copy of any supporting material they have found on the WWW that they intend to use in a manuscript or speech. That way you have a record of where you found the supporting material that can be provided to your instructor upon request.

The most effective student speeches and papers we have encountered have used supporting material to make compelling arguments, clearly explain important concepts, and elicit emotional reactions from readers and listeners. This level of effectiveness cannot be reached without planning, effort and creativity with respect to gathering and using support material. We hope the tips in this chapter aid you in your search for effective support material whether that journey be through a dusty book stack or cyberspace.

CHAPTER FIVE

APPENDIX A
Model Paper Following <u>MLA</u> Guidelines

Southwest Airline: LUV in the Air

Julie Price

Communication 336

Dr. John Bourhis

10 May 1998

APPENDIX A

Southwest Airlines: LUV in the Air

The planes are on time. The customers are happy and satisfied. The management trusts the employees and amply rewards them for going above and beyond the call of duty. The employees love to go above and beyond that call of duty and take great care and pride in their jobs. Because of these characteristics, Southwest Airlines is an organization out of the ordinary. At Southwest, nothing is impossible, and everything can be based on love. Even their monthly newsletter, LUV Lines reflects this attitude. Headquartered in Dallas, Texas at Love Field, Southwest employs over 20,000 people. Regarded as one of the top airlines in the business, Southwest takes customer service very seriously. In fact, Southwest is the only airline ever to win the Triple Crown award (Frieberg and Frieberg 8). The Triple Crown is given to the airline with the "best on-time service, fewest customer complaints, and smallest number of mishandled bags" (Frieberg and Frieberg 205). The executive officers of Southwest expect nothing but the best from their employees -- and themselves. The stories of these executive officers and the business of Southwest itself show customers why Southwest is one of the top airlines in the world today. But to fully understand Southwest Airlines, there are some aspects that must be explored as well. Southwest Airlines, like many organizations, is defined by its history, human relations methods, culture and organizational assimilation.

The Southwest idea was born in late 1966. Rollin King, a businessman

from San Antonio, and his partner, John Parker, decided there needed to be a

"small commuter air service ... [because it was] inconvenient and expensive to

travel between Houston, Dallas, and San Antonio" (Frieberg and Frieberg 14).

King then called his friend Herb Kelleher, a lawyer also in San Antonio. King

and Kelleher met for drinks and King explained the idea. Their conversation

consisted of, "Herb, let's start an airline." "Rollin, you're crazy. Let's do it!"

(Frieberg and Frieberg 15). The concept was to provide service to the big

Texas cities at the lowest cost possible. With the idea planted in their heads, it

was impossible to escape after that. King and Kelleher set to work to make

their idea become a reality, but they ran into more obstacles than they had

originally anticipated. For instance, there were several other airlines already

serving the Houston-Dallas-San Antonio areas. King and Kelleher took the

other airlines to court so they could fly too. But "Braniff, Continental, and

Texas International argued that the market Southwest wanted to serve was

already saturated, that there was no room for another carrier ... The trial court

ruled that Dallas, Houston, and San Antonio were adequately served by the

existing carriers and that the cities Southwest proposed to enter could not

support a new carrier" (Frieberg and Frieberg 17). Southwest appealed that

decision twice, but it was upheld both times. Finally, Kelleher proposed that

they "go one more round with them" (Frieberg and Frieberg 17). The Texas

Supreme Court overturned the previous decisions and Southwest could finally

fly. King and Kelleher set to work with another new partner, Lamar Muse,
buying airplanes, raising money and finding employees (Frieberg and Frieberg
19). However, the battle against the other airlines was not over. Kelleher
headed back to the Texas Supreme Court to get a restraining order from
Braniff and Texas International thrown out (Frieberg and Frieberg 20).
Kelleher called Muse to tell him to let the planes fly. "When Muse confided
that he was still concerned about the sheriff showing up to enforce the
injunction, Kelleher didn't mince any words: 'I told Lamar, you roll right over
the son of a bitch and leave our tire tracks on his uniform if you have to'"
(Frieberg and Frieberg 21).

While King and Kelleher were the brains behind the beginning of
Southwest, there were many others helping out behind the scenes. One such
influential person was Colleen Barrett, Kelleher's legal secretary. Barrett had
the kind of spirit Southwest needed to get off the ground, Kelleher said.
"Barrett is willing to try almost anything once and is responsible for bringing
many new ideas to the company" (Frieberg and Frieberg 113). Barrett has
since been promoted to executive vice-president of customers and a corporate
secretary. Bill Franklin was another important person in the success of
Southwest Airlines. He came to Southwest in the beginning from a rival airline
and was made vice president of ground operation. It is because of Franklin that
Southwest was able to do their famous "ten-minute turn." This meant that a

plane spent only ten minutes at the terminal before it was sent back up in the air. Because Southwest had only three planes in the beginning, the ten-minute turn was important to keep as many flights going as possible. Franklin recognized this necessity and put it into action. "Franklin ... was a man of action, a no-nonsense, get-it-done type of guy" (Frieberg and Frieberg 34). Franklin told his station managers and employees that it would be done -- or else. In fact, Franklin actually told a Houston station manager,

> We're going to do ten-minute turns with this airplane. If you
> can't do a ten-minute turn, then you're going to get fired and
> we'll bring in somebody else. If he can't do a ten-minute
> turn, we'll fire him, too. And we'll just keeping firing until
> we can find someone who can do it! (Frieberg and Frieberg
> 34)

A distinguishing characteristic of Southwest is that employees are the most important asset. When Southwest first took flight in 1971, it employed approximately 200 people. Today, approximately 20,000 people work for Southwest around the United States. But even today, a debt is owed to those original employees, Kelleher believes. "Their determination was the fuel that inspired the intense work ethic and esprit de corps that drive Southwest today" (Frieberg and Frieberg 36). In fact, 36 of those original 200 employees are still with Southwest today. Southwest makes sure it takes care of employees. For example, at Southwest, unlike most businesses, the customers don't come first -- the employees do. This is an important philosophy at Southwest because Kelleher believes that "when the systems, structure, policies, procedures, and practices of an organization are designed and lived out so that employees genuinely feel that they come first ... they are not skeptical or apprehensive when management says, 'Do what you think is right- (Frieberg and Frieberg 282). Southwest allows employees the freedom of making decisions when the time comes. They trust the work force enough to depend on them to make the right decision based on their own judgment. "'We never jump on employees for leaning too far in the direction of the customer,' says Colleen Barrett. 'They have to know that we stand behind them, and we do'" (Frieberg and Frieberg 287). Even the hiring strategies at Southwest stress the value of employees. one of the hiring mottoes at Southwest is "'Professionals, need not apply" (Frieberg and Frieberg 64). Kelleher, in fact, hates the terms professional and businesslike. Kelleher says: "Anybody who likes to be called a 'professional, probably shouldn't be around Southwest Airlines"(Frieberg and Frieberg 65). Instead, Southwest looks for people who want to have fun and who have good people skills. And while employees are expected to be nothing but the best, Southwest always makes sure employees have fun too. Southwest loves to celebrate any and every occasion, but celebrations of milestones are most important. "The difference between Southwest Airlines and many other companies may be that when the hunger to celebrate is felt, particularly after a stunning victory, rather than ignore it or avoid it, Southwest nourishes it" (Frieberg and Frieberg 177). Employees have the opportunity to relax and have a good time with their coworkers. Southwest takes great care in making sure employees are happy and taken care of because in the eyes of the business, when an employees is happy and taken care of, customers will be happy and taken care of too.

Southwest Airlines is a one-in-a-million company. Anymore, it seems it is very rare to find a company that began with so little, but managed to build itself into a top corporation. Southwest has done this by putting employees first, believing in the impossible and working as hard as possible. With such accomplishments as the Triple Crown already in their possession, Southwest Airlines has shown the world what it takes to be a top airline. In fact, Southwest attributes their outstanding service and accomplishments to their employees and the company is famous for the outstanding way they treat their employees.

Theories X and Y describe the way a company views its employees. Developed by Douglas McGregor, "'Theory X and Theory Y styles of management most clearly distinguishes the basic values of human relations theory" (Kreps 82). Theory X is based on distrust of employees while Theory Y relies more on the trust and goodwill of employees. According to McGregor, the three premises of Theory X are that(1) workers are basically lazy and irresponsible and cannot be trusted . . . (2) most people must be coerced, controlled, directed, threatened with punishment to get them to put forth adequate effort toward the achievement of organizational objectives . . . (3) [workers] also really do not want the opportunity to exercise responsibility and like to be told what to do by their supervisors (Kreps 82). Theory Y, on the other hand, has six basic assumptions about employees. Employers who base their management style on Theory Y believe, first of all, that workers can work hard if they want to and the more job satisfaction the employees have, the harder they will work in their jobs. Second, Theory Y believers think employees can be self-directed in accomplishing their objective. Third, employees will work to obtain personal fulfillment. Theory Y followers also believe that employees' willingness to take on job responsibility depends on their experiences within the company. Fifth, Theory Y-based companies believe employees can evaluate themselves and their co-workers better than management could because they are more directly involved in that area of work. Finally, Theory Y believers want to use their employees as resources of knowledge. This means that companies with a Theory Y foundation are willing to ask employees for their input on decisions (Kreps 84). In short, Theory Y companies believe in their employees. Employees are seen more as an asset rather than simply a work force. Employees are trusted and participate in management while in Theory X employees are left out of decision-making issues.

As much as a company can be, Southwest Airlines is based on Theory Y. Around the airline world, others know how much Southwest employees value their jobs and coworkers. Southwest is a perfect example of McGregor's Theory Y when it comes to human relations. At Southwest, employers do believe employees like to work because the employees tell them they like their jobs; Southwest knows self-control is possible because they see it in employees everyday; Southwest sees the employees being creative in problem solving and other aspects of their job; and Southwest allows employees to be self-directed. Southwest Airlines perfectly exemplifies Theory Y. Employee involvement in decision-making is a huge part of Theory Y. In a consultative approach to management, there is greater subordinate interaction (Bourhis, "Decision Making"). At Southwest Airlines, employees at all levels are directly involved in decision making. Southwest even allows employees to make their own decisions, even if those decisions go against some rules. For instance, one Christmas Eve, an elderly gentleman appeared at the ticket counter in the Los Angeles International Airport and needed to go to New Orleans. However, there were no more flights to New Orleans that night. The man had nowhere else to go. Rachel Dyer, a customer service agent, took it upon herself to help the man. She helped him get a room for the evening as well as meal tickets. As Dyer said, "It's not that I think that ... as a company we could even afford to do for everyone what we did in this situation. ... I am so proud and happy to work for a company that not only allows but encourages me to help people who are really in need" (Frieberg and Frieberg 226). Dyer was later commended by her superiors on her great decision. When Dyer went back to thank her supervisor, Kathy Hooper, for giving her the ability to make the decision, Hooper just smiled and said, "I love stories like that'" (Frieberg and Frieberg 226). In fact, Dyer's story is often used as an example of the love and compassion Southwest believes employees should show to customers. Her decision made an impact on the company. At some companies, she might have been reprimanded for becoming so involved with a customer. However, at Southwest, Dyer had the flexibility of the company rules to do what she thought was right in that specific situation. Southwest believes that some rules need to be broken in certain circumstances. They believe employees have the knowledge and self-direction to know when those rules need to be bent, or even broken in order to make the correct decision.

In another example of Theory Y, Southwest encourages employees to be creative and to develop their own ideas. For instance, "in 1985, after just three years with Southwest, Matt Buckley ... proposed an idea that he was convinced would revolutionize the industry and catapult his career at the same time. The idea was a same-day, door-to-door cargo product called RUSH PLUS" (Frieberg and Frieberg 131). At Southwest, Buckley was able to develop an idea he thought would help Southwest and himself. He dealt with little

resistance from his superiors. As Buckley remembered, "I'll never forget

getting the nod from Herb when he said, 'Let's try it!'" (Frieberg and Frieberg

131). However, even when Buckley's idea did not turn out as he had expected,

he still dealt with few problems. Southwest had devoted much money to

Buckley's idea in hopes that it would generate more money. But it did not.

RUSH PLUS was determined to be a failure within a few months after it

began. Buckley remembers, "As far as I was concerned, my life was over and

the headstone read, 'Here Lies a Failure. RUSH PLUS Was Not Hot. Nor Was

It Happenin'" (Frieberg and Frieberg 132). Still Buckley was not even

reprimanded for losing company money. In fact, Buckley has been promoted

several times since the RUSH PLUS failure. At Southwest, what Buckley

learned from his bad decision meant more than just the failure. "First, the

company values his entrepreneurial spirit and enthusiasm. Second, Buckley

was able to turn a failure into an opportunity for personal growth and maturity.

... mistakes teach us a lot about ourselves and the methods we use for getting

things done" (Frieberg and Frieberg 133). Southwest encourages Buckley and

other employees to be creative and to pursue their own ideas and dreams, even

if some of those ideas and dreams do not turn out for the best.

Southwest Airlines is a perfect example of McGregor's Theory Y. At

Southwest, the employers believe in their employees and their employees

return that trust. Southwest exemplifies every characteristic of a Theory Y organization, from allowing employees to be self-directed to using employees as resources of knowledge. While this is mainly a human relations focus, it is also an example of Southwest's culture.

The culture of an organization is an important idea for potential employees to look at before accepting or even applying for a job with a company. The culture of an organization can explain how and why things are done in an organization, as well as the way employees act at the company. When new employees enter an organization, they can be mystified by what is going on before them. As Michael Pacanowsky and Clifford Geertz observed, "Organizational culture is not just another piece of the puzzle; it is the puzzle ... The only way to reduce the puzzlement is to observe as if one were a stranger in a foreign land" (Griffin 246). So that is what many new employees resort to: observing to see how things are done around the organization before becoming directly involved. New employees can observe both external and internal signs of culture. External indicators include the company's mission statement, community involvement and advertisements. Internal signs of culture can involve the way other employees dress, the leadership, the stories and myths of the company as well as the rites, rituals and ceremonies of the organization (Bourhis, "Culture"). As new employees observe these indicators, they pick up on basic information about the company -- information that is important to know in order for them to survive at the company.

For employees entering the Southwest Airlines company, the culture is very easy to learn. There are several underlying themes about the culture that potential employees must know, however. First of all, at Southwest, loyalty is rewarded. Those employees who have been with Southwest since the beginning are an honored group. Secondly, employees have to be willing to do things in uncommon ways. Ideas and personal thoughts are a relished commodity at Southwest. Finally, casual is the ruling idea at Southwest. If employees are uncomfortable in their uniforms, Southwest believes they cannot make their customers comfortable either. But these are easy ideas to see upon arrival at Southwest. Not only is it very apparent upon first glance, but other employees are more than willing to share stories about their experiences with the company.

As far as external indicators, Southwest's advertisements are an excellent signifier of the culture there. Frequently, advertisements are designed to honor employees as a way of attracting customer attention. For example, during Southwest's twenty-fifth anniversary year, several advertisements were run to thank original employees. One advertisement in particular honored those workers who are the "behind the scenes" workers: mechanics, clerks and supervisors rather than the top people of the organization or the flight attendants and pilots the customers see regularly. The advertisement showed six men looking upwards to the sky. The caption honored the men and threw in a bit of humor as well: "After 25 years it's nice to take a step back and admire what you've accomplished. Our aircraft maintenance team has always

kept our fleet in top operating form. We have as much pride in them as they

have in their jobs. To these six original employees we would like to say

thanks. Okay guys. Break's over" (Frieberg and Frieberg 104). Other

advertisements are run simply to show the world the culture Southwest really

values. In a recruitment advertisement for Southwest, a picture of a dinosaur

had been colored by Brian, an elementary-aged child. The dinosaur was

colored in purples, greens, oranges, reds -- every color of the rainbow. What is

even more catching about the advertisement is that Brian had not stayed inside

the lines when he was coloring. A note from his teacher attached to the picture

read, "Brian - Please try to color inside the lines!" The headline of the

advertisement explained, "Brian Shows an Early Aptitude for Working at

Southwest Airlines." The body copy that followed elaborated even more:

"Wouldn't you know it. The one who gave Miss Canfield the most trouble

ended up working at Southwest Airlines. And he fit in quite nicely, thank you

very much. You see, at Southwest Airlines, you get check pluses for . . .

coloring outside the lines" (Frieberg and Frieberg 70). Southwest allows the

advertisements to show the world the relaxed and calm culture they have

worked to create.

 As far as internal indicators of culture at Southwest, there are several. The

stories the employees tell are a terrific sign of Southwest's culture, as is the way employees dress. The employees of Southwest take it upon themselves to share the stories of Southwest's culture as well. They tell the stories of how the company has supported them through tough times and good times. They tell the stories of the elaborate celebrations that happen at the company when a goal is achieved. And the employees love the stories because they are a part of them. The employees are a part of the culture of Southwest. For example, Southwest pilot Terry Millard had been with the company for two years when he was diagnosed with cancer. After he had been out of work for three months, Millard and his wife "received a big package from Herb and Colleen. It was a big cheesecake and some dooda dooda stuff and it was the first major representation that in this company nobody is forgotten" (Frieberg and Frieberg 163). But that was not all Southwest did for Millard. He recovered from one surgery, but later had to take another leave of absence. Again, he was remembered, and Millard was moved by the compassion of the company. "When I was out the second time . . . the same thing happened, different package . . . the company cared enough to put in place all of the expense and resources to make it happen we are continually blown away" (Frieberg and Frieberg 163). Such stories definitely show the culture of Southwest Airlines.

The way the employees of Southwest dress reflects the culture as well. On a Southwest flight, customers will never see a flight attendant in a stuffy suit or dress. Instead, polos and khaki shorts or pants are the norm. In fact, when the company first began in the early 1970s, the uniforms for flight attendants included "hot pants and white high-heeled go-go boots" (Frieberg and Frieberg 38). While that was shocking but still acceptable in the 1970s, Southwest eventually decided the uniforms needed a change, but they still wanted to keep the casual and fun aspect. The uniforms became "'fun wear' -- casual clothing [for] customer service agents working the gates to executives at headquarters" (Frieberg and Frieberg 204). The customers love the casual attire the employees wear on flights. In fact, at one point when Southwest did have a more formal uniform that included a jacket, skirts or pants and ties, customers actually complained. "Customers commented that with the more formal uniform the flights weren't as fun and the flight attendants didn't seem as playful and friendly" (Frieberg and Frieberg 205). Even more than uniforms, however, the culture of Southwest is obvious even to customers of the airline because the employees willingly reflect the culture the organization sets for them. As Southwest passenger Michelle Fullen said in a letter written to Kelleher, "[The two flight attendants] were the best I've ever seen. Professional, friendly, and sincere. ... You can tell when someone actually likes their job and meeting people. It was the kind of service you can't teach or force" (Frieberg and Frieberg 272).

Southwest Airlines takes organization culture very seriously, yet their culture is fun-loving and relaxed. In fact, Southwest takes culture so seriously, they make sure everyone knows their culture -- including their customers. In fact, culture is one of the first things new employees learn during organizational assimilation as well. organizational assimilation is yet another important aspect for the person who is joining a new company. New employees need to know how things are done at the company. To do this, they use organizational assimilation. According to Dr. John Bourhis ("Learn Culture"), "organizational assimilation is the process by which culture is learned." There are two main parts of organizational assimilation: organizational indoctrination, which is when the organization executives tell the employees what the expectations are, and organizational socialization, which is more informal because it is the employees talking to each other, rather than to the executives (Bourhis, "Decision Making"). In addition, there are four main steps to organizational assimilation. They include anticipatory assimilation, encounter, adaptation and exit (Bourhis, "Assimilation"). In other words, new employees address the expectations they have about the company, they have their actual first experiences with the company, they adapt and then they finally exit the organization after becoming a part of it. It is their way of learning and becoming a part of the organization. For many organizations, much of the assimilation takes place through organizational socialization, or the casual phase. As Kevin Barge, David Schlueter and Angel Hachtel of Baylor University found, memorable messages have a direct influence in this area. In their research, they found "memorable messages provide information regarding the norms, values, expectations, rules, requirements, and rationality of the organizational culture" (Barge, Schlueter and Hachtel 4). In light of the various ways organizational assimilation can take place, it is a very important idea for new employees to look at.

At Southwest Airlines, organizational assimilation depends quite a bit on the "memorable messages" the scholars of Baylor University discussed. But the messages are not just spoken messages -- they are found in the way veteran employees act and in the way new employees are hired. When new employees see the old employees going out of their way to help a co-worker in order to make the company itself look better, a message is sent. Southwest makes sure the employees have the freedom to do whatever it takes to make everything go smoothly, even if it involves a pilot helping the grounds crew. For example, a photograph in Nuts! Southwest Airlines' Crazy Recipe for Business and Personal Success shows a pilot helping a member of the grounds crew. The caption reads, "It's not unusual to see pilots giving ramp agents a hand or vice presidents handling baggage" (Frieberg and Frieberg 89). Such activities send a message to new employees. In their own way of organizational assimilation, Southwest shows employees that helping out is not only good for everyone, it is expected of everyone.

However, a big part of organizational assimilation can take place at Southwest Airlines even before people are hired. The way Southwest hires new employees is definitely a way prospective employees learn the culture of

Southwest. But Southwest executives also use the hiring process to make sure

they get the right type of people working for them. For example, Southwest

prides itself on not adhering to the usual stuffy uniform. So when a group of

eight men were applying for pilot positions and they were asked to take off

their dark suits and put on Bermuda shorts instead, it sent a message. The

applicants saw that Southwest was a fun and relaxed company. "Six of the

applicants accepted the offer and interviewed for the rest of the day in suit

coats, black dress shoes and socks, and Bermuda shorts. They were hired"

(Frieberg and Frieberg 68). But those doing the hiring at Southwest received a

message as well. Southwest hires people with good attitudes -- "an intangible

quality in people that cases them to want to do whatever it takes and to want to

go that extra mile whenever they need to" (Frieberg and Frieberg 69).

Southwest uses the hiring process to teach prospective employees

organizational assimilation in the best way possible.

Southwest Airlines is a one-in-a-million organization. There are very few

organizations in the world today that have so much trust and dependence in

their employees. With such executives as Herb Kelleher and Colleen Barrett

who do their best to do what is right and to go above and beyond the call of

duty, it only makes sense for them to expect the same from their employees.

They care about their employees and it shows to the rest of the world.

Customers notice how care free, yet attentive the flight attendants and pilots

are. The attitudes of Southwest employees are based on several things: the freedom of the casual uniform, the great leadership they have, the way they all seem to love their jobs just because they do or the way in which they were hired and introduced to the Southwest way of life. Whatever these attitudes are based on, it is working and has worked for over twenty-five years. Southwest began with nothing. The hard work of many people -- Kelleher and Barrett included -- made it the success it is today. Southwest is undoubtedly the top airline of the decade and it shows no signs of slowing down any time soon.

Works Cited

Barge, Kevin, David Schlueter, and Angel Hachtel. "Memorable messages and newcomer socialization." Speech Communication Association of America, November, 1994, New Orleans.

Bourhis, John. "Participative Decision Making Theory." Southwest Missouri State University. Springfield, 12 Sept. 1998.

—. "Culture." Southwest Missouri State University. Springfield, 29 Sept. 1998.

—. "How to Learn an Organization's Culture." Southwest Missouri State University. Springfield, 13 Oct. 1998.

—. "A Model of Organizational Assimilation." Southwest Missouri State University. Springfield, 1 Nov. 1998.

Frieberg, Kevin, and Jackie Frieberg. NUTS! Southwest Airlines: Crazy recipe for business and personal success. Austin: Board Press Inc, 1996.

Griffin, Emily. A First Look at Communication Theory. 3rd ed. New York: McGraw-Hill Companies, 1997.

Kreps, Gary. (1990). Organizational Communication: Theory and Practice. 2nd ed. New York: Longman, 1990.

APPENDIX B
Model Paper Following <u>APA</u> Guidelines

Running head: THE CULTURE OF SOUTHWEST AIRLINES

Southwest Airlines: LUV in the Air

Julie Price

Southwest Missouri State University

APPENDIX B

Southwest Airlines: LUV in the Air

The planes are on time. The customers are happy and satisfied. The management trusts the employees and amply rewards them for going above and beyond the call of duty. The employees love to go above and beyond that call of duty and take great care and pride in their jobs. Because of these characteristics, Southwest Airlines is an organization out of the ordinary. At Southwest, nothing is impossible, and everything can be based on love. Even their monthly newsletter, <u>LUV Lines</u> reflects this attitude. Headquartered in Dallas, Texas at Love Field, Southwest employs over 20,000 people. Regarded as one of the top airlines in the business, Southwest takes customer service very seriously. In fact, Southwest is the only airline ever to win the Triple Crown award (Frieberg & Frieberg, 1996, p. 8). The Triple Crown is given to the airline with the "best on-time service, fewest customer complaints, and smallest number of mishandled bags" (Frieberg & Frieberg p. 205). The executive officers of Southwest expect nothing but the best from their employees -- and themselves. The stories of these executive officers and the business of Southwest itself show customers why Southwest is one of the top airlines in the world today. But to fully understand Southwest Airlines, there are some aspects that must be explored as well. Southwest Airlines, like many organizations, is defined by its history, human relations methods, culture and organizational assimilation.

The Southwest idea was born in late 1966. Rollin King, a businessman from San Antonio, and his partner, John Parker, decided there needed to be a "small commuter air service ... [because it was] inconvenient and expensive to travel between Houston, Dallas, and San Antonio" (Frieberg & Frieberg, 1996, p. 14). King then called his friend Herb Kelleher, a lawyer also in San Antonio. King and Kelleher met for drinks and King explained the idea. Their conversation consisted of, "Herb, let's start an airline." "Rollin, you're crazy. Let's do it!" (Frieberg & Frieberg, 1996, p. 15). The concept was to provide service to the big Texas cities at the lowest cost possible. With the idea planted in their heads, it was impossible to escape after that. King and Kelleher set to work to make their idea become a reality, but they ran into more obstacles than they had originally anticipated. For instance, there were several other airlines already serving the Houston-Dallas-San Antonio areas. King and Kelleher took the other airlines to court so they could fly too. But "Braniff, Continental, and Texas International argued that the market Southwest wanted to serve was already saturated, that there was no room for another carrier . . . . The trial court ruled that Dallas, Houston, and San Antonio were adequately served by the existing carriers and that the cities Southwest proposed to enter could not support a new carrier" (Frieberg & Frieberg, 1996, p. 17). Southwest appealed that decision twice, but it was upheld both times. Finally, Kelleher proposed that they "go one more round with them" (Frieberg & Frieberg, 1996, p. 17). The Texas Supreme Court overturned the previous decisions and Southwest

could finally fly. King and Kelleher set to work with another new partner,
Lamar Muse, buying airplanes, raising money and finding employees
(Frieberg & Frieberg, 1996, p. 19). However, the battle against the other
airlines was not over. Kelleher headed back to the Texas Supreme Court to get
a restraining order from Braniff and Texas International thrown out (Frieberg
& Frieberg, 1996, p. 20). Kelleher called Muse to tell him to let the planes fly.
"When Muse confided that he was still concerned about the sheriff showing up
to enforce the injunction, Kelleher didn't mince any words: 'I told Lamar, you
roll right over the son of a bitch and leave our tire tracks on his uniform if you
have to'" (Frieberg & Frieberg, 1996, p. 21).

While King and Kelleher were the brains behind the beginning of
Southwest, there were many others helping out behind the scenes. One such
influential person was Colleen Barrett, Kelleher's legal secretary. Barrett had
the kind of spirit Southwest needed to get off the ground, Kelleher said.
"Barrett is willing to try almost anything once and is responsible for bringing
many new ideas to the company" (Frieberg & Frieberg, 1996, p. 113). Barrett
has since been promoted to executive vice-president of customers and a
corporate secretary. Bill Franklin was another important person in the success
of Southwest Airlines. He came to Southwest in the beginning from a rival
airline and was made vice president of ground operation. It is because of
Franklin that Southwest was able to do their famous "ten-minute turn." This
meant that a plane spent only ten minutes at the terminal before it was sent

back up in the air. Because Southwest had only three planes in the beginning,

the ten-minute turn was important to keep as many flights going as possible.

Franklin recognized this necessity and put it into action. "Franklin ... was a

man of action, a no-nonsense, get-it-done type of guy" (Frieberg & Frieberg,

1996, p. 34). Franklin told his station managers and employees that it would be

done -- or else. In fact, Franklin actually told a Houston station manager,

> We're going to do ten-minute turns with this airplane. If you
>
> can't do a ten-minute turn, then you're going to get fired and
>
> we'll bring in somebody else. If he can't do a ten-minute
>
> turn, we'll fire him, too. And we'll just keeping firing until
>
> we can find someone who can do it! (Frieberg & Frieberg,
>
> 1996, p. 34)

A distinguishing characteristic of Southwest is that employees are the

most important asset. When Southwest first took flight in 1971, it employed

approximately 200 people. Today, approximately 20,000 people work for

Southwest around the United States. But even today, a debt is owed to those

original employees, Kelleher believes. "Their determination was the fuel that

inspired the intense work ethic and esprit de corps that drive Southwest today"

(Frieberg & Frieberg, 1996, p. 36). In fact, 36 of those original 200 employees

are still with Southwest today. Southwest makes sure it takes care of

employees. For example, at Southwest, unlike most businesses, the customers

don't come first -- the employees do. This is an important philosophy at

Southwest because Kelleher believes that "when the systems, structure, policies, procedures, and practices of an organization are designed and lived out so that employees genuinely feel that they come first . . . they are not skeptical or apprehensive when management says, 'Do what you think is right (Frieberg & Frieberg, 1996, p. 282). Southwest allows employees the freedom of making decisions when the time comes. They trust the work force enough to depend on them to make the right decision based on their own judgment. "'We never jump on employees for leaning too far in the direction of the customer,' says Colleen Barrett. 'They have to know that we stand behind them, and we do'" (Frieberg & Frieberg, 1996, p. 287). Even the hiring strategies at Southwest stress the value of employees. one of the hiring mottoes at Southwest is "Professionals, need not apply" (Frieberg & Frieberg, 1996, p. 64). Kelleher, in fact, hates the terms professional and businesslike. Kelleher says: "Anybody who likes to be called a 'professional, probably shouldn't be around Southwest Airlines"(Frieberg & Frieberg, 1996, p. 65). Instead, Southwest looks for people who want to have fun and who have good people skills. And while employees are expected to be nothing but the best, Southwest always makes sure employees have fun too. Southwest loves to celebrate any and every occasion, but celebrations of milestones are most important. "The difference between Southwest Airlines and many other companies may be that when the hunger to celebrate is felt, particularly after a stunning victory, rather than ignore it or avoid it, Southwest nourishes it" (Frieberg & Frieberg, 1996,

p. 177). Employees have the opportunity to relax and have a good time with their coworkers. Southwest takes great care in making sure employees are happy and taken care of because in the eyes of the business, when an employees is happy and taken care of, customers will be happy and taken care of too.

Southwest Airlines is a one-in-a-million company. Anymore, it seems it is very rare to find a company that began with so little, but managed to build itself into a top corporation. Southwest has done this by putting employees first, believing in the impossible and working as hard as possible. With such accomplishments as the Triple Crown already in their possession, Southwest Airlines has shown the world what it takes to be a top airline. In fact, Southwest attributes their outstanding service and accomplishments to their employees and the company is famous for the outstanding way they treat their employees.

Theories X and Y describe the way a company views its employees. Developed by Douglas McGregor, 'Theory X and Theory styles of management most clearly distinguishes the basic values of human relations theory" (Kreps, 1990, p. 82). Theory X is based on distrust of employees while Theory Y relies more on the trust and goodwill of employees. According to McGregor, the three premises of Theory X are that(1) workers are basically lazy and irresponsible and cannot be trust ... (2) most people must be coerced, controlled, directed, threatened with punishment to get them to put forth adequate effort toward the achievement of organizational objectives ... (3)

[workers] also really do not want the opportunity to exercise responsibility and

like to be told what to do by their supervisors (Kreps, 1990, p. 82). Theory Y,

on the other hand, has six basic assumptions about employees. Employers who

base their management style on Theory Y believe, first of all, that workers can

work hard if they want to and the more job satisfaction the employees have,

the harder they will work in their jobs. Second, Theory Y believers think

employees can be self-directed in accomplishing their objective. Third,

employees will work to obtain personal fulfillment. Theory Y followers also

believe that employees' willingness to take on job responsibility depends on

their experiences within the company. Fifth, Theory Y-based companies

believe employees can evaluate themselves and their co-workers better than

management could because they are more directly involved in that area of

work. Finally, Theory Y believers want to use their employees as resources of

knowledge. This means that companies with a Theory Y foundation are

willing to ask employees for their input on decisions (Kreps, 1990, p. 84). In

short, Theory Y companies believe in their employees. Employees are seen

more as an asset rather than simply a work force. Employees are trusted and

participate in management while in Theory X employees are left out of

decision-making.

   As much as a company can be, Southwest Airlines is based on Theory Y.

Around the airline world, others know how much Southwest employees value their jobs and coworkers. Southwest is a perfect example of McGregor's Theory Y when it comes to human relations. At Southwest, employers do believe employees like to work because the employees tell them they like their jobs; Southwest knows self-control is possible because they see it in employees everyday; Southwest sees the employees being creative in problem solving and other aspects of their job; and Southwest allows employees to be self-directed. Southwest Airlines perfectly exemplifies Theory Y.

Employee involvement in decision-making is a huge part of Theory Y. In a consultative approach to management, there is a greater subordinate interaction (Bourhis, 1998a). At Southwest Airlines, employees at all levels are directly involved in decision making. Southwest even allows employees to make their own decisions, even if those decisions go against some rules. For instance, one Christmas Eve, an elderly gentleman appeared at the ticket counter in the Los Angeles International Airport and needed to go to New Orleans. However, there were no more flights to New Orleans that night. The man had nowhere else to go. Rachel Dyer, a customer service agent, took it upon herself to help the man. She helped him get a room for the evening as well as meal tickets. As Dyer said, "It's not that I think that ... as a company we could even afford to do for everyone what we did in this situation. ... I am so proud and happy to work for a company that not only allows but encourages me to help people who are really in need" (Frieberg & Frieberg, 1996, p. 226). Dyer was later commended by her superiors on her great decision. When Dyer went back to thank her supervisor, Kathy Hooper, for giving her the ability to

make the decision, Hooper "just smiled and said, I love stories like that"

(Frieberg & Frieberg, 1996, p. 226). In fact, Dyer's story is often used as an

example of the love and compassion Southwest believes employees should

show to customers. Her decision made an impact on the company. At some

companies, she might have been reprimanded for becoming so involved with a

customer. However, at Southwest, Dyer had the flexibility of the company

rules to do what she thought was right in that specific situation. Southwest

believes that some rules need to be broken in certain circumstances. They

believe employees have the knowledge and self-direction to know when those

rules need to be bent, or even broken in order to make the correct decision.

In another example of Theory Y, Southwest encourages employees to be

creative and to develop their own ideas. For instance, "in 1985, after just three

years with Southwest, Matt Buckley . . . proposed an idea that he was

convinced would revolutionize the industry and catapult his career at the same

time. The idea was a same-day, door-to-door cargo product called RUSH

PLUS" (Frieberg & Frieberg, 1996, p. 131). At Southwest, Buckley was able

to develop an idea he thought would help Southwest and himself. He dealt

with little resistance from his superiors. As Buckley remembered, "I'll never

forget getting the nod from Herb when he said, "Let's try it!"" (Frieberg &

Frieberg, 1996, p. 131). However, even when Buckley's idea did not turn out

as he had expected, he still dealt with few problems. Southwest had devoted

much money to Buckley's idea in hopes that it would generate more money.
But it did not. RUSH PLUS was determined to be a failure within a few
months after it began. 'Buckley remembers, 'As far as I was concerned, my life
was over and the headstone read, 'Here Lies a Failure. RUSH PLUS Was Not
Hot. Nor Was It Happenin''" (Frieberg & Frieberg, 1996, p. 132). Still
Buckley was not even reprimanded for losing company money. In fact,
Buckley has been promoted several times since the RUSH PLUS failure. At
Southwest, what Buckley learned from his bad decision meant more than just
the failure. "First, the company values his entrepreneurial spirit and
enthusiasm. Second, Buckley was able to turn a failure into an opportunity for
personal growth and maturity. ... mistakes teach us a lot about ourselves and
the methods we use for getting things done" (Frieberg & Frieberg, 1996, p.
133). Southwest encourages Buckley and other employees to be creative and
to pursue their own ideas and dreams, even if some of those ideas and dreams
do not turn out for the best.

Southwest Airlines is a perfect example of McGregor's Theory Y. At
Southwest, the employers believe in their employees and their employees
return that trust. Southwest exemplifies every characteristic of a Theory Y
organization, from allowing employees to be self-directed to using employees
as resources of knowledge. While this is mainly a human relations focus, it is
also an example of Southwest's culture.

The culture of an organization is an important idea for potential

employees to look at before accepting or even applying for a job with a

company. The culture of an organization can explain how and why things are

done in an organization, as well as the way employees act at the company.

When new employees enter an organization, they can be mystified by what is

going on before them. As Michael Pacanowsky and Clifford Geertz observed,

"Organizational culture is not just another piece of the puzzle; it is the puzzle .

. . The only way to reduce the puzzlement is to observe as if one were a

stranger in a foreign land" (Griffin, 1997, p. 246). So that is what many new

employees resort to: observing to see how things are done around the

organization before becoming directly involved. New employees can observe

both external and internal signs of culture. External indicators include the

company's mission statement, community involvement and advertisements.

Internal signs of culture can involve the way other employees dress, the

leadership, the stories and myths of the company as well as the rites, rituals

and ceremonies of the organization (Bourhis, 1998b). As new employees

observe these indicators, they pick up on basic information about the company

-- information that is important to know in order for them to survive at the

company.

For employees entering the Southwest Airlines company, the culture is

very easy to learn. There are several underlying themes about the culture that

potential employees must know, however. First of all, at Southwest, loyalty is rewarded. Those employees who have been with Southwest since the beginning are an honored group. Secondly, employees have to be willing to do things in uncommon ways. Ideas and personal thoughts are a relished commodity at Southwest. Finally, casual is the ruling idea at Southwest. If employees are uncomfortable in their uniforms, Southwest believes they cannot make their customers comfortable either. But these are easy ideas to see upon arrival at Southwest. Not only is it very apparent upon first glance, but other employees are more than willing to share stories about their experiences with the company.

As far as external indicators, Southwest's advertisements are an excellent signifier of the culture there. Frequently, advertisements are designed to honor employees as a way of attracting customer attention. For example, during Southwest's twenty-fifth anniversary year, several advertisements were run to thank original employees. One advertisement in particular honored those workers who are the "behind the scenes" workers: mechanics, clerks and supervisors rather than the top people of the organization or the flight attendants and pilots the customers see regularly. The advertisement showed six men looking upwards to the sky. The caption honored the men and threw in a bit of humor as well: "After 25 years it's nice to take a step back and admire what you've accomplished. Our aircraft maintenance team has always kept our fleet in top operating form. We have as much pride in them as they have in their jobs. To these six original employees we would like to say thanks. Okay guys. Break's over" (Frieberg & Frieberg, 1996, p. 104). Other

advertisements are run simply to show the world the culture Southwest really

values. In a recruitment advertisement for Southwest, a picture of a dinosaur

had been colored by Brian, an elementary-aged child. The dinosaur was

colored in purples, greens, oranges, reds -- every color of the rainbow. What is

even more catching about the advertisement is that Brian had not stayed inside

the lines when he was coloring. A note from his teacher attached to the picture

read, "Brian - Please try to color inside the lines!" The headline of the

advertisement explained, "Brian Shows an Early Aptitude for Working at

Southwest Airlines." The body copy that followed elaborated even more:

"Wouldn't you know it. The one who gave Miss Canfield the most trouble

ended up working at Southwest Airlines. And he fit in quite nicely, thank you

very much. You see, at Southwest Airlines, you get check pluses for . . .

coloring outside the lines" (Frieberg & Frieberg, 1996, p. 70). Southwest

allows the advertisements to show the world the relaxed and calm culture they

have worked to create.

As far as internal indicators of culture at Southwest, there are several. The

stories the employees tell are a terrific sign of Southwest's culture, as is the

way employees dress. The employees of Southwest take it upon themselves to

share the stories of Southwest's culture as well. They tell the stories of how the

company has supported them through tough times and good times. They tell

the stories of the elaborate celebrations that happen at the company when a goal is achieved. And the employees love the stories because they are a part of them. The employees are a part of the culture of Southwest. For example, Southwest pilot Terry Millard had been with the company for two years when he was diagnosed with cancer. After he had been out of work for three months, Millard and his wife "received a big package from Herb and Colleen. It was a big cheesecake and some dooda dooda stuff and it was the first major representation that in this company nobody is forgotten" (Frieberg & Frieberg, 1996, p. 163). But that was not all Southwest did for Millard. He recovered from one surgery, but later had to take another leave of absence. Again, he was remembered, and Millard was moved by the compassion of the company. "When I was out the second time . . . the same thing happened, different package . . . the company cared enough to put in place all of the expense and resources to make it happen we are continually blown away" (Frieberg & Frieberg, 1996, p. 163). Such stories definitely show the culture of Southwest Airlines.

The way the employees of Southwest dress reflects the culture as well. On a Southwest flight, customers will never see a flight attendant in a stuffy suit or dress. Instead, polos and khaki shorts or pants are the norm. In fact, when the company first began in the early 1970s, the uniforms for flight attendants included "hot pants and white high-heeled go-go boots" (Frieberg & Frieberg, 1996, p. 38). While that was shocking but still acceptable in the 1970s, Southwest eventually decided the uniforms needed a change, but they still wanted to keep the casual and fun aspect. The uniforms became "'fun wear' -- casual clothing [for] customer service agents working the gates to executives at headquarters" (Frieberg & Frieberg, 1996, p. 204). The customers love the casual attire the employees wear on flights. In fact, at one point when Southwest did have a more formal uniform that included a jacket, skirts or pants and ties, customers actually complained. "Customers commented that with the more formal uniform the flights weren't as fun and the flight attendants didn't seem as playful and friendly" (Frieberg & Frieberg, 1996, p. 205). Even more than uniforms, however, the culture of Southwest is obvious even to customers of the airline because the employees willingly reflect the culture the organization sets for them. As Southwest passenger Michelle Fullen said in a letter written to Kelleher, "[The two flight attendants] were the best I've ever seen. Professional, friendly, and sincere. ... You can tell when someone actually likes their job and meeting people. It was the kind of service you can't teach or force" (Frieberg & Frieberg, 1996, p. 272).

Southwest Airlines takes organization culture very seriously, yet their culture is fun-loving and relaxed. In fact, Southwest takes culture so seriously, they make sure everyone knows their culture --- including their customers. In fact, culture is one of the first things new employees learn during organizational assimilation as well. organizational assimilation is yet another important aspect for the person who is joining a new company. New employees need to know how things are done at the company. To do this, they

---

use organizational assimilation. According to Dr. John Bourhis (1998c), "organizational assimilation is the process by which culture is learned." There are two main parts of organizational assimilation: organizational indoctrination, which is when the organization executives tell the employees what the expectations are, and organizational socialization, which is more informal because it is the employees talking to each other, rather than to the executives (Bourhis, 1998a). In addition, there are four main steps to organizational assimilation. They include anticipatory assimilation, encounter, adaptation and exit (Bourhis, 1998d). In other words, new employees address the expectations they have about the company, they have their actual first experiences with the company, they adapt and then they finally exit the organization after becoming a part of it. It is their way of learning and becoming a part of the organization. For many organizations, much of the assimilation takes place through the organizational socialization, or the casual phase. As J. Kevin Barge, David W. Schlueter and Angel Hachtel of Baylor University found, memorable messages have a direct influence in this area. In their research, they found "memorable messages provide information regarding the norms, values, expectations, rules, requirements, and rationality of the organizational culture" (Barge, Schueter, and Hachtel, 1994, p. 4). In light of the various ways organizational assimilation can take place, it is a very important idea for new employees to look at.

At Southwest Airlines, organizational assimilation depends quite a bit on the "memorable messages" the scholars of Baylor University discussed. But the messages are not just spoken messages --- they are found in the way veteran employees act and in the way new employees are hired. When new employees see the old employees going out of their way to help a co-worker in order to make the company itself look better, a message is sent. Southwest makes sure the employees have the freedom to do whatever it takes to make everything go smoothly, even if it involves a pilot helping the grounds crew. For example, a photograph in <u>Nuts! Southwest Airlines' Crazy Recipe for Business and Personal Success</u> shows a pilot helping a member of the grounds crew. The caption reads, "It's not unusual to see pilots giving ramp agents a hand or vice presidents handling baggage" (Frieberg & Frieberg, 1996, p. 89). Such activities send a message to new employees. In their own way of organizational assimilation, Southwest shows employees that helping out is not only good for everyone, it is expected of everyone.

However, a big part of organizational assimilation can take place at Southwest Airlines even before people are hired. The way Southwest hires new employees is definitely a way prospective employees learn the culture of Southwest. But Southwest executives also use the hiring process to make sure they get the right type of people working for them. For example, Southwest prides itself on not adhering to the usual stuffy uniform. So when a group of eight men were applying for pilot positions and they were asked to take off their dark suits and put on Bermuda shorts instead, it sent a message. The applicants saw that Southwest was a fun and relaxed company. "Six of the applicants accepted the offer and interviewed for the rest of the day in suit coats, black dress shoes and socks, and Bermuda shorts. They were hired" (Frieberg & Frieberg, 1996, p. 68). But those doing the hiring at Southwest received a message as well. Southwest hires people with good attitudes --- "an intangible quality in people that cases them to want to do whatever it takes and to want to go that extra mile whenever they need to" (Frieberg & Frieberg, 1996, p. 69). Southwest uses the hiring process to teach prospective employees organizational assimilation in the best way possible.

Southwest Airlines is a one-in-a-million organization. There are very few organizations in the world today that have so much trust and dependence in their employees. With such executives as Herb Kelleher and Colleen Barrett who do their best to do what is right and to go above and beyond the call of duty, it only makes sense for them to expect the same from their employees. They care about their employees and it shows to the rest of the world. Customers notice how care free, yet attentive the flight attendants and pilots are. The attitudes of Southwest employees are based on several things: the freedom of the casual uniform, the great leadership they have, the way they all seem to love their jobs just because they do or the way in which they were hired and introduced to the Southwest way of life. Whatever these attitudes are based on, it is working and has worked for over twenty-five years. Southwest began with nothing. The hard work of many people -- Kelleher and Barrett

included -- made it the success it is today. Southwest is undoubtedly the top

airline of the decade and it shows no signs of slowing down any time soon.

References

Barge, K., Schlueter, D., & Hachtel, A. (1994, November). Memorable messages and newcomer socialization. Paper presented at the annual conference, Speech Communication Association, New Orleans.

Bourhis, J. (1998a, September 15). Participative decision making theory. Southwest Missouri State University. Springfield, MO.

Bourhis, J. (1998b, September 29). Culture. Southwest Missouri State University. Springfield, MO.

Bourhis, J. (1998c, October 13). How to learn an organization's culture. Southwest Missouri State University. Springfield, MO.

Bourhis, J. (1998d). A model of organizational assimilation. Southwest Missouri State University. Springfield, MO.

Frieberg, K. & Frieberg, J. (1996). NUTS! Southwest Airlines: Crazy recipe for business and personal success. Austin: Board Press Inc.

Griffin, E. (1997). A first look at communication theory (3rd ed.). New York: McGraw-Hill Companies.

Kreps, G. (1990). Organizational communication: Theory and practice (2nd ed.). New York: Longman.

APPENDIX C
Model Annotated
Bibliography

Running head: LONELINESS AND MASS MEDIA USE

Loneliness and Mass Media Use: An Annotated Bibliography

Jane Doe and John Doe

Southwest Missouri State University

Loneliness and Mass Media Use

Austin, A. (1984). Loneliness and the attributes of movie-going.

<u>Psychological Reports, 55,</u> 223-227.

This study examined how loneliness is related to various movie-going

attributes. Four-hundred-and-eighty-three college students randomly selected

from a Midwestern university ranging in ages from 16 to 36 years old

participated. A questionnaire using the Revised UCLA Loneliness Scale,

demographic items, and questions relating to movie going attendance was

given to the students. The movie attendance questions asked about the pattern

of movie attendance, whether they went on a regular basis or in streaks, how

far in advance they made their decisions about going to the movies, and

whether they went to the movies alone or in a group. Using the UCLA scale,

three types of loneliness were defined: intimate (a feeling of isolation), social

(a sense of not having a social network), and affiliation (the feeling of not

belonging). The results showed no significant difference between the three

types of loneliness and the pattern and frequency of movie-going. There was a

pattern discovered between the type of loneliness and the size of the group

attending the movies. Those who had a feeling of "not belonging" attended

movies in smaller groups. The overall results of the study suggested few

differences between lonely and less lonely college students and movie-going

patterns. According to this study loneliness did not bring about more regular

movie attendance.

Austin, A. (1985). Loneliness and use of six mass media among college

students. Psychological Reports, 56, 323-327.

This study examined the relationship between loneliness and mass media

consumption among college students. Four-hundred-and-eighty-three college

students ranging in age from 16 to 36 years old participated. The students were

given a questionnaire containing the Revised UCLA Loneliness Scale,

demographic questions and questions pertaining to their use of mass media,

including television, movies, newspapers, magazines, radio and books

(excluding textbooks). Overall, the results indicated little relationship between

loneliness and frequency of media use. The authors concluded that students

may use alternative methods to relieve loneliness other than increasing mass

media consumption, which include the built in sociability of college life and

the responsibilities associated with classwork.

Elliott, W., & Quattlebaum, C. (1979). Similarities in patterns of media

use. The Western Journal of Speech Communication, 43, 61-92.

The purpose of this study was to determine the consequences of media use

sought by media users. A questionnaire was developed which examined eight

different media and the relative strength of the specific medium in relation to

the individual's specific needs or reasons for using a specific media. The

questionnaire should determine how eight media were used in the satisfaction of ten gratification items. Of the 259 subjects completing the questionnaires, males made up 61.2% of the sample and females 38.8%. Results indicate that two major patterns in media use are: (1) people use media as a means to maintain contact with society and (2) people use media to fulfill individual needs. The researchers concluded that television was the most generally satisfactory medium. Books, film, and recorded music showed parallel patterns of need satisfaction with one interpersonal medium, friends. Media appear to function differently in need satisfaction. Availability, cost, and involvement may also be factors in media differentiation.

Finn, S., & Gorr, M. (1988). Social isolation and social support as correlates of television motivations. Communication Research, 5, 135-158. This study examined the relationship between motivations for television viewing and personality differences. The students were selected from the University of North Carolina over a three year period. Approximately 96 students were selected each year to create a panel demographically similar to the undergraduate student population. Once a week, the students were interviewed and responded with yes/no answers into a computer. The students were asked questions pertaining to loneliness, shyness and interpersonal support as well as television viewing habits. The researchers divided motives into two headings with loneliness, shyness, habit, and companionship falling under the heading of "social compensation," and relaxation, entertainment, and arousal under "mood management." The hypothesis was students with strong social skills would react positively to viewing habits under "mood

management" and those with weak social skills would react positively with

"social compensation" viewing habits. The study supported their hypothesis. It

also found that as level of social support increased, so did the level of

television viewing for mood management.

Kubey, R. (1986). Television use in everyday life: coping with

unstructured time. Journal of Communication, 36, 108-123.

The purpose of this study was to observe any relationships between subjective

experience occurring in particular domains of daily life and an individual's

level of television viewing. One hundred subjects (54% males, 63% females)

employed full-time at five companies in the Chicago area participated in the

study. Examination of the moods in which TV viewing is embedded should

lead to greater success in establishing when and why people watch television.

This study was conduct on site, not in the laboratory. These experiments

employ experience sampling, a method that allows for the study of the total

range of reportable moods, thoughts, and behaviors as they occur in normal

daily experience. Each respondent carried a "paper" or "beeper." Subjects are

"beeped" seven to nine times per day. After being signaled, each respondent

filled out a Random Activity Information Sheet (RAIS) which asked questions

concerning basic mood and activity. Results indicated particular kinds of experience (moods) occurring among certain kinds of people (e.g., less privileged and divorced and separated persons) and under certain conditions (solitary and un-structured time) can explain particular uses of media (heavy television viewing). When people from less affluent, less educated, less privileged, and divorced or separated demographic groups feel bad in unstructured or solitary situations and television is available, they are generally more inclined to watch than are more affluent, more educated, more privileged and married respondents. This study concluded that feeling bad in unstructured and solitary times leads to an increase use of television.

Lull, J. (1986). Social use of television. Human Communication Research, 6, 197-209.

This study explored the nature of social uses which audience members make of television. More than 200 families, representing blue-collar, white-collar, and farm types were studied. This study utilized a participant observational methodology (ethnography) as the means for data collection. The ethnographic methodology consisted of (1) participant observation, (2) the use of informants, and (3) in-depth interviewing. Observers looked for regularity in communicative acts reflected in interpersonal roles and relationships associated with the use of mass media. Social uses of television in the home are of two types: structural and relational. Two components of structural uses are environmental (background noise, companionship, entertainment) and regulative (punctuation of time and activity talk patterns). The associated components of the relational dimension are communication facilitation, affiliation/avoidance, social learning, competence/dominance. This study concluded that it may be very helpful to make inferences on the basis of the four major divisions of the relational dimension in order to rationalize specific "viewer types" or "family types." This may allow the individual to determine if a person or family uses television intentionally for the facilitation of effective family communication; for the potential to construct the desired degree of interpersonal affiliation; for learning about how to behave in the social world; or for demonstrating competence or dominating others in the viewer group.

Perloff, R., Quarles, R., & Drutz, M. (1988). Loneliness, depression and the use of television. Journalism Quarterly, 60, 353-356.

This study assessed the impact of the situational constraint of social isolation and depression on the uses of television by college students. One hundred and fifty urban university students ages 18-26 in an introductory mass communication course were surveyed. Respondents filled out a questionnaire including questions on dating, number of friends, dissatisfaction with relationships, and depression. They were also asked the extent to which they watched television to relieve boredom or to escape from problems. The results showed dating involvement only impacted television viewing due to the amount of free time the student had. Depression did not affect television time.

Depression did have a modest impact on the viewer's involvement with television characters, but not the amount of television they watched. For television viewing time, subjective dispositions had a stronger impact than did situational variables, and situational variables affected the media variables indirectly through the dispositional variables.

Perse, E., & Rubin, A. (1990). Chronic loneliness and television use. Journal of Broadcasting & Electronic Media, 34, 37-53.

This article contains two studies investigating the relationship between chronic loneliness and television use. One study examined loneliness and local news viewing, the other loneliness and soap opera viewing. In the first study 380 non-traditional students enrolled in evening classes at a Midwest university completed a self-administered questionnaire. Twenty questions were from the UCLA Loneliness Scale to measure loneliness, the rest were viewing motive questions from previous research. The study found no substantial differences between the non-lonely and chronically lonely students in their media use, other than the chronic lonely tend to listen more to the radio. They also found lonely people watch news to pass the time rather than for informational or entertainment purposes. In the second study, 460 undergraduate students at a large midwestern university completed a self-administered questionnaire. Three hundred and twenty-eight reported they watched soap operas, with 68.9% being female. They were asked questions from the UCLA Loneliness Scale to measure loneliness and were asked questions about interpersonal channels and their reasons for watching their favorite daytime soap operas.

Ninety-one percent of those identified as chronically lonely watched television

on a more regular basis. Sixty-three percent of those identified as chronically

lonely were less involved in the soap operas compared to those who were

identified as not lonely. The conclusion was the chronically lonely primarily

use television to pass the time and don't become involved in what they are

watching. They do not use the media as a substitute for social interaction.

Rubin, A., Perse, E., & Powell, R. (1985). Loneliness, parasocial

interaction, and local television news viewing. Human Communication

Research, 12, 155-180.

This study examined the relationship between loneliness and the level of

parasocial interactions. Hypotheses were developed predicting parasocial

interaction from both a social interaction need due to loneliness and

instrumental television use. Questionnaires were completed by 329 persons

(65% females, 38% male). Questionnaires were administered during class

periods to 390 persons enrolled in 26 evening sections on two regional

campuses. A total of 339 respondents (86.9%) indicated that they watched

local television news. The subjects' loneliness levels were measured with the

revised UCLA Loneliness Scale. Results indicated that loneliness and

interpersonal communication channel use are negatively related. Loneliness and television reliance are positively related. Ritualized news viewing to fill

excess free time was related to more television viewing. Conclusions were that

individuals linked psychological need to media use and its outcomes.

Parasocial interaction can fulfill a social need for interaction and a major

determinant of parasocial interaction is a function of an individual's level of

loneliness. This study has developed a reliable empirical measure of parasocial

interaction to measure feelings of audience relationships with local television

news personalities.

Turow, J. (1974). Talk show radio as interpersonal communication.

Journal of Broadcasting, 18, 171-179.

This study investigates the use of broadcasting as a substitute for traditional

forms of interpersonal communication. This study was conducted at a

Philadelphia-based radio station. Calls coming to the "talk jockey" were

screened, allowing brief interviews with callers concerning their motives for

calling, their attitudes towards society (as measured by the Strole Anomia

Scale). Basic demographic information was also obtained. As a group, the

callers appeared to be more geographically isolated and less mobile than the

general population. Callers tended to be over 60 years of age and came from

lower socio-economic class. A large number of the callers were chronically ill

or invalids. The over-whelming majority of the callers welcome the interactive

contact the talk show provided, along with the interactive dimension combined

with the anonymity of the telephone. This study concluded that talk show radio callers are motivated to dial the station out of need for interpersonal

contact rather than out of a desire to incite social reform.

APPENDIX D
Model Journal Critique

Running head: CAUSAL MODELING OF CA

Causal Modeling of Communication Apprehension: A Journal Critique

John Doe

Southwest Missouri State University

Causal Modeling of Communication Apprehension: A Journal Critique

Source

Beatty, M., Dobos, J., Balfantz, G., & Kuwabara, A. (1991).

Communication apprehension, state anxiety and behavioral disruption: A

causal analysis. Communication Quarterly, 39, 48-58.

Purpose

The authors attempt to map out the causal relationship, if any, among

communication apprehension, state anxiety, and behavioral disruption.

Communication apprehension is defined as "the predisposition to avoid

communication, if possible, or suffer a variety of anxiety-type feelings"

(Beatty, Dobos, Balfantz, & Kuwabara, 1991, p. 48). In contrast, state anxiety

refers to "the reaction experienced during actual communication" (Beatty et

al., 1991, p. 48). Behavioral disruption is used to refer to those observable

behaviors that are manifested as a result of communication apprehension and

state anxiety: trembling, stammering, and low verbal output (Beatty et al.,

1991).

Communication apprehension may trigger behavioral disruption, but is the

converse true? Can behavioral disruption lead to the development and/or

maintenance of communication apprehension? Previous research has shown

"strong evidence for this causal relationship between these variables" (Beatty

et al., 1991, p. 49). Applying these concepts to a public speaking scenario, "communicators are apprehensive because they observe themselves behaving in an anxious manner" (Beatty et al., 1991, p. 50). From this the speaker predisposes him/herself to exhibit a disruptive behavioral pattern. This pattern reinforces communication apprehension which in turn reinforces the state anxiety situation which originally was a causal factor in the behavioral disruption. The purpose of this study was to observe the interactive relationship(s) among the three variables in question and to apply interactive models to explain communication apprehension theory.

Rationale

If behavioral responses are a result of the interaction rather than a cause, then behavioral responses may not be the necessary observable element for the study of communication apprehension. Communication apprehension represents the pre-interactive environment and state anxiety represents the actual interactive situation. State anxiety should be a better determinate of behavioral disruption than communication apprehension. Research in this area would contribute to a greater understanding of communication apprehension.

Methodology

The authors empirically tested the following three specific hypotheses:

H1: The coefficient for the path from communication apprehension to behavior should be significant;

H2: The coefficient for the path from state anxiety to behavior should be

   significant; and

H3: The coefficient for the path from behavior to communication should

   be significant. (Beatty et al, 1991, p. 49)

Communication apprehension was measured using the six item public

speaking subscale of McCroskey's Personal Report of Communication

Apprehension-24. Prior research has established adequate validity of the

measure with a reliability coefficient of .80. This makes the PRCA-24

subscale an adequate measure of the construct.

   A similar procedure was used to measure state anxiety using the State

Anxiety Inventory. Prior research has established adequate validity of the

measure with a reliability coefficient of .80. This makes the state anxiety scale

an adequate measure of the construct.

   The observable assessment of speaker behavior was quantified using the

Behavioral Assessment of Speech Anxiety Scale. The reliability coefficient of

the measure was judged acceptable by the authors.

   To eliminate any temporal bias, data were collected at two points in time

and structural models representing potential relationships between

communication apprehension, state anxiety, and behavioral disruption were

formulated. Analysis was used to accept or reject the models based on the

statistical significance of the data obtained.

The PRCA-6 was given to seventy-three undergraduates prior to each of two oral performances. Five weeks elapsed between each administration of the measure. Structured oral interpretations rather than a less-structured extemporaneous style was the required method of delivery used in this study.

The resulting data was categorized according to total BASA (Behavioral Assessment of Speech Anxiety) score for trial one and trial two using statistical correlations between behavioral categories and total BASA scores observed.

Results

Statistical analysis implied that neither the path coefficient from communication apprehension to behavior or the path from state anxiety to behavior were statistically significant at the .05 level. These findings did not support either of the first two hypotheses.

In the second causal model, communication apprehension was the dependent variable. Results supported hypothesis three at the .05 level of significance. A significant path coefficient was observed for state anxiety. The path coefficient for BASA scores was also statistically significant at the .05 level.

The overall conclusions suggest that the hypothesized three-variable causal model with communication apprehension as the dependent variable best fits the observed data.

Evaluation

Study in the area of communication apprehension is applied not only to the structured environment of public speaking, but also has broad theoretical scope which would apply to areas of interpersonal, small group, and organizational communication. This area of inquiry applies to events or situations that happen frequently; it is a powerful construct.

One potential weakness of the study is the use of BASA as the measurement of speaker behavior. This is a purely subjective analysis of an untrained observer who is required to observe specific categorical behaviors for one minute per behavioral category. I question whether this instrument is conducive to the establishment of definitive observation suitable for qualitative analysis with valid statistical inference. A more appropriate alternative might be to videotape speakers and have them evaluated by trained professionals who are more qualified and less likely to make a subjective analysis of the experimental subjects.

A second potential weakness is the statistical procedures employed in the study. I would recommend an alternative statistical analysis based upon the multiple linear regression model. This technique is used to explain or predict the behavior of a certain dependent variable using more than one possible causal factor. For example, mean scores were used on the BASA evaluation which lend themselves nicely to analysis of variance. The authors could have used analysis of variance to explain which factor(s) had a significant effect on the variables of interest.

From a heuristic perspective this study has merit, but I would like to evaluate data with alternative statistical procedures and utilize different measurement and assessment criteria. I remain unconvinced that questions concerning causal relationships between communication apprehension, state anxiety, and behavior can be conclusively answered given the methods in this study.

In terms of validity, the study does help to explain some interesting interaction within the communication process of path analysis and performance anxiety. I do have some problems with generalizability based on what I believe to be limitations in the study's methodology.

The study does meet the criteria for being parsimonious. The authors, from their point of view, consider these causal relationships quite conclusive and essentially simple and straightforward. In my opinion, however, this must be tempered with the concerns already expressed regarding the methodological limitations inherent in the study's design.

Conclusion

This study addressed some extremely relevant and powerful topics. When these ideas are constrained within the school of empirical analysis, much is lost. If laboratory techniques were used, I would combine physiological observation of anxiety related reactions such as heart rate, respiration, galvanic skin response, and blood pressure.

APPENDIX E
Model Review of Literature

Running head: PERSONAL ADVERTISEMENTS

An Analysis of the Use of Newspaper Personal Advertisements for

Initiating Interaction

Jane Doe

Southwest Missouri State University

An Analysis of the Use of Newspaper Personal Advertisements

for Initiating Interaction

Samuel Johnson once wrote that "Promise, large promise, is the soul of an advertisement." Samuel Johnson's summation of the nature of advertising still holds true today, not only for the want ads of everyday commerce, but also for the personal advertisement in which advertisers hold forth the promise of friendship or romance. Just as modern marketing practices seek to tailor persuasive efforts to target audiences, many singles now seek to selectively communicate their availability and desirability through advertisements read by other singles. Whether in a 'lonely hearts' section of national tabloids, the personals section of metropolitan dailies, or in singles tabloids or magazines, the personal advertisement is clearly an attempt to initiate significant interaction with others. The personals ad is a candidate for scholarly attention because such advertising is a widely available form of initial interaction in the development of relationships (Foxman, 1982). Although researchers have studied the content of ads, there has been little study of their use and the interaction that follows from them. The purpose of this study is to explore the use of personal ads, rather than their content. A review of the content analysis of personals, the popular literature on personals, and the sole previous survey-based study of personals will precede the reporting of a survey of writers of personals advertisements.

Prior research on the phenomenon of newspaper personals advertisements has utilized content analysis methodologies to study the influence of gender and sexual orientation on the content of personal ads. The theoretical bases for these efforts have been the social desirability hypothesis (i.e., that people seek mates with similar levels of social desirability) and exchange theory (i.e., seeking a mate is a bargaining exchange; people seek to present themselves optimally, and to seek a mate with traditional role characteristics to exchange). Bolig, Stein and McKenry (1984), Cameron, Oskamp, and Sparks (1977), and Harrison and Saeed (1977) examine male-female differences in personal ad content.

Laner (1978), Laner and Kevi Kamel (1977), and Lumby (1978) focus on the influence of sexual orientation on ad content. Deaux and Hanna (1984) examine both gender and sexual orientation influences. Lee's (1976) content analysis of homosexual ads is one exception to this pattern of research; Lee attempts to demonstrate a typology of styles of love relationships.

In one of the earliest content analysis studies of personals, Harrison and Saeed (1977) tested the social desirability hypothesis. They found a traditional pattern of matching in a sample of 800 ads from a weekly national tabloid. In this pattern women were more likely to offer attractiveness, seek security, question the motives of respondents, and seek an older meanwhile men were more likely to offer security, profess interest in marriage, and seek a younger woman. Cameron, Oskamp, and Sparks (1977) found a similar pattern of content in ads placed by heterosexuals in a regional singles newspaper.

Laner (1978) found lesbian ads to be more like ads placed by heterosexual women than like ads placed by homosexual or heterosexual men. Ads placed by lesbian women tended toward an androgynous orientation, in contrast to the virilization of ads placed by gay men found in the Laner and Levi Kamel (1978) and Lumby (1978) studies.

Deaux and Hanna (1984) examined both heterosexual and homosexual ads. Their results supported the earlier findings of traditional role exchanges for heterosexuals. for lesbian women, physical characteristics were de-emphasized; interests, hobbies, and goals for the relationship were emphasized. Homosexual men placed a greater stress on physical appearance.

Lynn and Shurgot (1984) combined content analysis with a correlational analysis of the number of responses garnered by ads. They found that advertisers who assured attractiveness received more responses than those who placed ads without such assurances. Content analysis provides a basis for understanding the characteristics of advertisements, but does not shed light on the use of ads; for example, we cannot know from this research why advertisers choose this form of initiation or how meeting through the ads may influence relationship development. The sole exception to the content analysis approach is an unpublished study by Lundeberg and Walfort (1988). They surveyed a small number (47) of writers of personals. In addition to demographic information, they were interested in how the initiation of a relationship through a personal advertisement might alter traditional role behavior. While the small non-random sample makes it difficult to generalize from their results, the authors suggested that the demographics of writers of ads and the characteristics of ad-initiated relationships are conventional.

The popular literature has also attended to the personals phenomenon. The case studies in magazines have been generally favorable in their reviews of the use of personals (Finn, 1983; McMahon, 1979). Foxman (1982) reported her own extensive experience writing ads, providing composition tips and examples of response letters she had received. The popular literature is largely restricted to a human-interest approach of "gee whiz, isn't this interesting and unusual?" While it provides a glimpse of the realm of personals, it is based on anecdotal evidence.

Three exploratory questions guided the present survey based study of the use of personals ads:

Q1 Who are the advertisers?

Q2 What are the advertiser's objectives and outcomes?

Q3 What are the conventions in the use of personals ads?

Content analysis cannot provide adequate answers to these questions. The limited space in an ad limits the amount of information provided on advertiser demographics and objectives. The conventions and outcomes of ad use are not part of ad content. A survey allows the writers of ads to provide more complete demographic information and to discuss their experiences of the conventions and outcomes of the use of personals.

> The preceding is an excerpt from a much longer paper. The full text of the paper includes a complete list of references as required in APA.

APPENDIX F
Student Exercises

Your Name: _____ Date _____

Chapter 1 Exercise 1

There are at least ten citation errors in the following list of Works Cited. None of the errors are spelling, grammatical or spacing. Circle each error in the following list and provide a correction. Turn the corrected list of Works Cited in to your professor as instructed.

Works Cited

Aldinger, C. "Pentagon Justifies Attack." <u>ABC News.com</u>. 1 Sept. 1999.

    <http://www.abcnews.go.com/go/sections/world/DailyNews/kosovo_main

    _990515.html>.

Bourhis, John. <jsb806f@mail.smsu.edu> <u>Updating the Style Manual</u>.

    Personal email. 1 June 1999. Sept. 29, 1999.

"Call It Cybernoia." Philadelphia Daily News, March 1, 1997, p. 11.

Harnack, Andrew, and Kleppinger, Eugene. <u>Online! A Reference Guide to

    Using Internet Sources</u>. New York: St. Martin's.

Johannesen, R. Ethics in Human Communication, 4th ed. Prospect Heights:

    Waveland Press, 1996.

Nichols, M. <u>The Lost Art of Listening</u>. Prentice-Hall, 1995.

Raymond, Kelly. "Toward a New Tolerance: Gun Control and Community

    Policing." <u>Vital Speeches</u> 60 (1993): 332-334.

Wolvin, Andrew, and Carolyn Coakley. <u>Listening</u>, 6th ed. Dubuque: Brown

    and Benchmark, 1995. 223-396.

Your Name: _____ Date _____

Chapter 1 Exercise 2

Based on the information presented in Chapter 1, answer the following
questions by writing the best answer in the space provided. For each question,
write "T" for true or "F" for false.

_____1. MLA stands for Modern Linguistic Association.

_____2. MLA style requires that you include a formal title page for every
paper you submit for evaluation.

_____3. When using a direct quotation, MLA requires that you provide the
reader with a page reference for locating the material quoted.

_____4. You should seriously consider justifying the right margin of your
manuscript because it makes the manuscript look more professional.

_____5. It is generally a good idea to keep a Xerox copy of any written work
you submit for evaluation for your personal files.

_____6. MLA style requires that you always double-space.

_____7. Proper pagination in MLA consists of your last name and the page
number in the upper right hand corner of the paper.

_____8. All scholarly writing submitted for evaluation requires pagination.

_____9. The first page of a MLA manuscript is the first page on which the text
of the manuscript appears.

_____10. In MLA, the list of works cited appears at the end of the paper.

Your Name: _____ Date _____

Chapter 2 Exercise 1

There are at least ten errors in the following list of references. Circle each error in the following list and provide a correction. Turn the corrected list of references in to your instructor.

REFERENCES

Adams, C. A. (1991). <u>Influences on the production and evaluation of regulative messages: Effects of social cognition, situational, and experiential variables in communication between hospital supervisors and volunteers</u>. Unpublished doctoral dissertation: University of Kansas.

Applegate, J. L. (1990). Constructs and communication: A pragmatic integration. In R. Neimeyer & G. Neimeyer (eds.), <u>Advances in personal construct psychology, Vol. 1</u> (pp. 197-224). Greenwich, CT: JAI.

Applegate, J. L., Burke, J. A., Burleson, B. R., Delia, J.G., and Kline, S. L. (1985). Reflection-enhancing parental communication. In I. E. Siegel (Ed.), <u>Personal belief systems: The psychological consequences for children</u> (pp. 107-142). Hillsdale, NJ: Erlbaum.

Bingham, S. G., & Burleson, B. R. (1988). Multiple effects of messages with multiple goals. <u>Human Communication Research, 16,</u> pp.184-216.

Bonhoeffer, D. (1954). <u>Life Together</u> (J.W. Doberstein, Trans.). San Francisco: Harper San Francisco.

Burgoon, M. (1995). A Kinder, Gentler Discipline: Feeling Good About Being Mediocre. In B. Burelson (Ed.), Communication yearbook 18 (pp. 464-479). Thousand Oaks, CA: Sage.

Burleson, B.R. (1989). The constructivist approach to person-centered communication: Analysis of a research exemplar. In Dervin, B, Grossberg, L, O'Keefe, B. & Wartellam E. (Eds.), Rethinking Communication: Vol. 2. Paradigm Exemplars (pp. 29-46). Newbury Park, CA: Sage.

Cheney, G. (1995). Democracy in the workplace: Theory and practice from the perspective of communication. Journal of Applied Communication Research, 23, 167-200.

Your Name: _____ Date _____

Chapter 2 Exercise 2

The following pages from a sample paper contain at least ten errors in APA style. Circle each error and provide a correction. Turn the corrected pages in to your professor as instructed.

Running Head: Supervising Volunteers

SUPERVISING VOLUNTEERS:

INFLUENCES ON THE LOGIC OF MESSAGES DESIGNED TO REGULATE BEHAVIOR

Carey Adams

Southwest Missouri State University

Gregory J. Shepherd

University of Kansas

Supervising Volunteers:

Influences on the Logic of Messages Designed to Regulate Behavior

Volunteerism is an important facet of American society. From de Tocqueville's praise of the volunteer spirit of 19th century America to George Bush's "thousand points of light," volunteerism has been recognized as a virtue in American culture and has been repeatedly called upon in the service of individual and social needs. A recent survey estimated that 80 million American adults donated 19.5 billion hours of service through volunteer efforts in a single year (Ilsley, 1990). Hospitals have traditionally been among the institutions that rely most heavily upon the services of volunteers. Indeed, recent cuts in federal funding have forced social services to rely more heavily on volunteer efforts than ever before (Rosentraub), and hospitals have been steadily expanding their volunteer programs to extend volunteer responsibilities beyond distributing magazines, delivering flowers, and visiting patients (see, for example, the model programs detailed in Developing an older volunteer program, 1981).

The increasing demand for volunteer services in hospitals has led to concern about the retention of volunteer staff in such organizations. A growing body of research has examined questions of volunteer satisfaction (e.g., Paradis, 1987, Lee & Burden, 1990). Not surprisingly, Mausner has shown that the quality of a volunteer's experience is closely related to the quality of the relationship that volunteer enjoys with the supervisory staff of the organization (1988). And, given the wealth of research that has suggested the quality of communication in superior-subordinate relationships is a good predictor of job satisfaction generally (Downs & Hazen, 1976; Pincus, 1986; Clampitt & Downs, 1987; Clampitt & Girardi, 1987), it is not it is not surprising to find that staff/volunteer relationships figure prominently in volunteer retention and satisfaction.

Your Name: _____ Date _____

Chapter 5 Exercise 1

Chapter 5 discussed several issues related to source evaluation. In particular, suggestions were provided concerning steps you should take when researching a topic. Primarily, those suggestions related to steps in finding supporting material, steps in evaluating supporting material, and steps in selecting supporting material. Below are several terms and concepts from the chapter. For each term, provide a brief definition/explanation based on what you read.

1.   External Consistency:

2.   Internal Consistency:

3.   Descriptive Statistics:

4.   Suffix (in WWW addresses e.g., .com, .org, .gov):

5.   Independent confirmation standard:

Your Name: _____ Date _____

Chapter 5 Exercise 2

Based on information presented in chapter 5, answer the following questions by writing the best answer in the space provided. For each question, write "T" for true or "F" for false.

____1.   You should review a minimum of 25 sources when preparing a manuscript or speech outline.

____2.   A researcher/speaker acts as the gatekeeper of information for your audience/reader.

____3.   Supporting material is generally more effective when it contains more technical terminology.

____4.   External consistency considers how consistent a source is with itself.

____5.   Personal interviews or e-mail messages are less verifiable than a book or magazine article.

____6.   It is appropriate to use unverifiable sources so long as other verifiable sources are included.

____7.   The example you choose to illustrate a concept should be typical of other examples for the concept.

____8.   In a speech, you should provide the qualifications of the sources you cite.

____9.   Descriptive statistics rely on data obtained from a sample.

____10. It is best to obtain independent confirmation before using any material from the WWW.

Your Name: _____ Date _____

Chapter 5 Exercise 3

In Chapter 5 we stressed the importance of carefully evaluating material obtained from the Internet. In this exercise, assume you are doing a research paper or presentation on sexual harassment in the workplace. Using an Internet search engine (your instructor may suggest a particular one), conduct a search for WWW material on this topic. First, provide the following information about the search you conducted:

1.   Exact search term/phrase you typed in: _____

2.   The search engine you used: _____

3.   The number of "hits" the search found: _____

Now, review your search results and find one government web site, one education web site, and one commercial web site. Provide the following information:

	WWW Address	Brief Description
Government Site		
Education Site		
Commercial Site		

Assuming that you could use only ONE of these sites in your project, which would you use and why?

Your Name: _____ Date _____

Chapter 5 Exercise 4

Although chapter 5 was primarily concerned with providing standards for source evaluation, suggestions were also provided concerning procedures for conducting searches for information on the WWW. For this exercise, assume you are planning an informative speech on environmental communication. Using Webcrawler (http://www.webcrawler.com), conduct the following searches and provide the indicated information (type the search terms exactly as shown):

Search 1:   Type in the following and conduct the search:
environmental communication

How many hits were returned?_____

What was the title of the first page listed?_____
_____

Search 2:   Type in the following and conduct the search:
+environmental +communication

How many hits were returned?_____

What was the title of the first page listed?_____
_____

Search 3:   Type in the following and conduct the search:
"environmental communication"

How many hits were returned?_____

What was the title of the first page listed?_____
_____

Which of these search terms provided the most useful return and why?

Your Name: _____ Date _____

Chapter 5 Exercise 5

For this assignment you will need to find one WWW site related to the topic for your speech (or research paper). First, print out the home page for the web site – you will need to staple that printout to this sheet before handing it in. Below is a list of criteria for evaluating the source. Those criteria are based on the heuristics presented in Chapter 5. Rate the web page you found on each of the criteria by circling a number from 1 to 5 (where 1 indicates the source is very weak on that particular criterion and 5 indicates it is very strong). After rating your source, provide a brief explanation for your rating (use additional paper if necessary).

Criterion	Rating	Explanation
Clarity	1 2 3 4 5	
Consistency	1 2 3 4 5	
Verifiable	1 2 3 4 5	
Competence	1 2 3 4 5	
Unbiased	1 2 3 4 5	
Relevance	1 2 3 4 5	
Overall	1 2 3 4 5	